For You

Andreas Seidl

Handover of Power

Global Version

Volume 8: Planned Economy

Imprint

Bibliographic information of the German National Library:
The German National Library lists this publication in the
German National Bibliography; detailed bibliographic data
are available on the Internet at http://dnb.dnb.de.

© 2022 Dipl. Pol. Theodor Andreas Seidl

Cover: Christiane Ebrecht
Translation: DeepL, Cologne
Production and publishing: BoD – Books on Demand,
Norderstedt

ISBN: 978-3-7568-1338-4

Acknowledgements

My thanks go to my family and friends who have made me who I am today. Special thanks to all those who supported me in writing this book. I would like to thank all my classmates, teachers, fellow students, lecturers, demonstrators, activists, colleagues, companies and countries with whom I have had the privilege of sharing the experiences from which all the ideas in this book have emerged. I would like to thank the staff of Books on Demand for their kind helpfulness. I thank the citizens of Seligenstadt for the harmony and solidarity in which I was able to write.

Foreword

This policy concept contains a variety of proposals for possible political reforms. It can be peacefully and democratically adapted to any current political system of any state in the world, but also to political systems in families, clubs, associations or companies. Wherever humans make or submit to rules that manage living together, the following proposals can be helpful. Readers who find the proposals so helpful that they would like to implement them together with like-minded people can contact the author. The contact form on the last page can be used for this purpose.

Faults and defects

I ask for your understanding that this volume was not professionally proofread. I could only afford professional proofreading for the summary. Spelling errors and unfortunate phrasing may therefore occur. As soon as this volume has sold enough to pay for a professional proofreading, it will be done. After that, a new edition will be published.

English version

Please understand that this volume has been translated automatically. I could only afford a professional translation for the summary. Poor wording and spelling errors may therefore occur. In case of doubt, the German version shall prevail. As soon as this volume has sold enough to pay for a professional translation, it will be done. After that, a new edition will be published. It was more important to me that no one in the world should have an information advantage than individual translation errors in the complete work.

References
If something has been quoted directly, it is set in italics. If the headings contain footnotes, the sources for direct and indirect quotations apply in the chapter for which the heading stands. Otherwise, quotations or source references are directly at the word or at the end of the sentence or paragraph. This book contains parts of text based on the Federal Constitution of the Swiss Confederation of 18 April 1999 (as of 12 February 2017), abbreviated to BV[1] and the Constitution of the Canton of Bern of 6 June 1993 (as of 11 March 2015), abbreviated to KV[2] .
If the constitutional paragraph, or individual paragraphs thereof, are based in whole or in part on extracts from the BV or KV, this is indicated in a footnote. The references to the corresponding footnotes for constitutional paragraphs are usually found after the heading of the affected chapter and sometimes in the body of the text. Articles used in the Swiss constitutions are listed in the footnote with a number after the title of the constitutional paragraph. Example: §123 Sample title: BV Art.123, KV Art.123.
All internet sources are fully cited in the footnotes. They were last accessed on 30.09.2021. All literature sources are also listed in full in the footnotes.
All references to tasks undertaken by other ministries and described in more detail there are given in footnotes. Example: Model Ministry - 1.2.3 Model Chapter.
All footnotes are to be viewed in comparison to the respective source, so-called indirect quotations. Direct quotations are set in italics, but hardly ever occur. The source reference is intended to enable further investigation and to take copyright

---

1 This is not an official publication. Only the publication by the Swiss Federal Chancellery is authoritative. https://www.fedlex.admin.ch/eli/cc/1999/404/de On 14.12.2021
2 This is not an official publication. The Bernese Official Collection of Laws is authoritative. https://www.belex.sites.be.ch/frontend/versions/2420?locale=de#ART71 On 16.12.2021

into account.

Table of contents

1 Goals of the Ministry of Planned Economy

In the four economic forms, the planned economy represents a life of security and modesty, but with maximum leisure time and minimum work. The democratisation of all subsystems is paramount. Residents should manage their Social Villages as independently and democratically as possible and work towards a self-sufficient existence in the overall network of all Social Villages.

The goal of Planned Economy is not to maximise profits, but to maximise leisure time and standard of living. The goal is achieved with an increase in productivity through innovation. Achieving living standards with all the amenities of the market economy is not the goal. The goal is to fulfil one's own needs plan, which was established by the majority in the needs assessment. Foreign trade with other economic forms should be balanced. A surplus is allowed, a deficit is forbidden. Insofar as the Planned Economy is dependent on taxpayers' money, that is at the time of its introduction and when the market economy abruptly produces mass unemployment.

Each village determines its own daily needs and can barter with the help of the other Social Villages to achieve a more suitable distribution of work and to be able to specialise. Revenues from the market economy aim to raise the standard of living of the village community through the purchase of innovative technology or expertise.

The basic goal is that all Social Villagers always have enough to eat, beds in warm and dry rooms, clothing, employment, fun, social contacts, medical care and educational opportunities. In order to reach the basic supply faster, the residents either have to work overtime or work more expediently.

The aim is also to enable as many Social Villagers as possible to realise their potential to work in their free time without having to rely on payment. Research and development becomes a leisure activity. Business ideas and inventions can be produced, tried out and marketed worldwide.

The aim of the Ministry of Planned Economy is to ensure that there is a labour market in the Social Villages that is self-sufficient and only relies on subsidies in exceptional cases. Economic policy issues concerning the supply of labour, goods and services are resolved in voting with the residents of the Social Village. This achieves the goal of finding a balance between work and leisure time that can guarantee basic supply at all times. The aim of the Planned Economy is to provide social security for all nationals and, if possible, also for citizens from Continental Union member states.

1.1 Improvements over the Soviet planned economy

In this Planned Economy, prices are flexible and adjusted to an internationally tradable currency. There are flexible exchange rates. In the Soviet Planned Economy, prices were often the same for decades. In the Planned Economy, both the workers themselves and the demanders are asked directly what they can afford or what they would like to afford. Although these negotiations take place on a regular annual basis, as in the Soviet Planned Economy, they are compared in real time by a computer programme during the course of the year, and if there are deviations of 10%, the working plan is automatically corrected. Neither in determining the work schedule does it make sense for the workers to lie and take more or less service, because all working hours are shared among all Social Villagers. Nor in the needs assessment does it make sense for the consumers to lie, because they are first allowed to wish for everything and immediately afterwards see how much free time it would cost them and whether they want to afford it. You don't have to ask for more to at least get what you would actually need. An algorithm automatically ensures that production is expanded or curtailed if a 10% deviation from the needs assessment is detected. The government in the form of politicians does not directly determine supply, demand or prices. Prices are no longer a control mechanism of the government, but are found in equilibrium by workers and consumers. Factors are scientifically formed that more accurately determine labour output per hour. Democratic governance, direct election of all politicians responsible for services in the Planned Economy and self-determination of Social Villagers at plenary assemblies, budget committees and needs assessments are also crucial.

2 Departments

The departments are divided into sub-departments and enumerations are usually considered as their individual units. Many tasks of some departments are completely taken over by other ministries as a service.

2.1 Central Department

Part of the Central Department is the Reception Office with the Courier and Mail Room, which directs all concerns, broadcasts and visitors to the appropriate place in the ministry.

2.1.1 Staff

The Human Resources Department is responsible for staff development and planning. For this purpose, it takes care of the recruitment of junior staff, intern and trainee programmes as well as the selection procedures for employees and special selection procedures for applicants with disabilities. For politicians and employees, the department prepares a job plan. In all its tasks, it works in voting with the personnel board.[1]

All other personnel matters are transferred to the respective ministries. The Ministry of Education is responsible for the training and further education of employees for the state service.[2] The Ministry of Labour takes over the service law.[3] This includes labour and collective bargaining law for employees in the state service, remuneration, personnel administration of all careers and employees, flexitime, holiday and sick leave, working time with or without flexitime in part-time or full-time at the place of work or in home work. The Ministry of Infrastructure provides housing assistance for all state employees.[4] The Ministry of Finance's Pay Office takes

---

1 Ministry of State Organisation - 2.1.1.1 Personnel board
2 Ministry of Education - 2.1.1.1 Education and training for the state service
3 Ministry of Labour - 4 State enterprises, 13 Labour Directory
4 Ministry of Infrastructure - 2.1.1.1 Housing assistance for state service employees

care of employees' salary, expenses, travel and relocation costs.[5] The Ministry of Education provides childcare for all employees in the state service.[6]

The Ministry of Health is responsible for the occupational health service.[7] It ensures occupational health management, deals with the treatment, education and prevention of occupational accidents, controls and provides occupational health and safety through the health auditors[8] of the Company Auditing Agency[9] .

2.1.2 Organisation

The ministries of media, security, justice, finance, labour, state organisation provide audit services for quality management in the ministry, evaluation of work performance, revenues and expenditures, as well as corruption prevention, sabotage protection and, if necessary, disciplinary matters.[10]

The language service for translating talks or texts is provided by the Ministry of Education.[11] The Ministry of Finance organises the annual budget vote and ensures proper accounting in each ministry.[12] It regulates budget procedures, budget law, staff budgets, departmental budgets, costs and cash management, and assists ministries in budget planning for the budget vote. The Ministry of Labour regulates procurement law and ensures corruption-free state orders and procurement.[13]

The Ministry of Digital Affairs supports the supply of Information Technology.[14] In voting with the Procurement Office of the Ministry of Labour, it takes care of the

---

5 Ministry of Finance - 2.1.1.1 Staff remuneration
6 Ministry of Education - 2.1.1.2 Childcare for employees in the state service
7 Ministry of Health - 2.1.1.1 Occupational Health Service
8 Ministry of Labour - 20.7.2 Health auditor
9 Ministry of Labor - 20 Company Auditing Agency
10 Ministries of Media, Security, Justice, Finance, State Organisation - 2.1.2.1 Audit services
11 Ministry of Education - 2.1.3 Language Service
12 Ministry of Finance - 8 state revenues, 9 state expenditure
13 Ministry of Labour - 6 Procurement Office
14 Ministry of Digital Affairs - 2.1.2.1.1 Supply of Information Technology

procurement, provision, maintenance and service of technical devices and software. Much of this is produced in-house to ensure data protection in information and communication technology. Information technology and digitalisation officers audit and advise the ministries. Digital appointment calendar and documentation services are provided as well as a digital policy archive including a library.

2.2 Management Department

The Management Department is the minister's department. With his office team, he provides policy planning and analysis for his ministry and coordinates the relationship between the nation and the municipality through exchanges with his deputies in the municipalities. He initiates cooperation with other ministries or citizens in committees and is supported by the Ministry of State Organisation.

The Ministry of Media Affairs, through its media service, provides press and public relations for the ministry, moderates civil dialogue, trains or provides a spokesperson for the minister, writes speeches and texts on request, and ensures the implementation of conferences and events.[15]

The Ministry of Digital Affairs is responsible for digital management and thus provides departmental management. It automatically produces business statistics, staff surveys and the current state of research through statistics. It automatically forwards proposals to the affected or empowered state employees. In document management, it ensures digitalisation and that ministries share forms with each other.[16]

2.3 Department for Social Villages

The Department for Social Villages organises plenary assemblies, committees and voting in Planned Economy in cooperation with the Ministries of State Organisation, Media and Digital Affairs. It operates the social directory[17]

---

15 Ministry of Media Affairs - 2.2.1.1 Media Service
16 Ministry of Digital Affairs - 2.1.2.1 Digital Service
17 Ministry of Digital - 12 Directories

and facilitates the use of the social card in cooperation with the Ministries of Finance, Integration and Digital Affairs. It oversees the operation of clubs and the activities of religious communities for compliance with the requirements of the Ministries of Family and Integration. In cooperation with the other ministries of economy, it determines the residence rights for the Planned Economy. With the People's Protection Service, the Company Auditing Agency and the People's Bank[18] , the move of persons, companies and finances into and out of the Planned Economy is organised.

2.4 Department for Economy and Enterprises

The Department for Economy and Enterprises coordinates economic cooperation between the Social Villages and with other economic forms. It monitors capacity utilisation and ensures equal burden sharing. It organises the needs assessments and, in cooperation with the Ministry of Digital Affairs, runs the computer programme to simulate needs and consumption, calculate prices and prepare the duty roster. In cooperation with the Company Auditing Agency, it analyses economic trends and proposes appropriate measures to the Minister for Planned Economy. In cooperation with the People's Bank, it ensures the operation of the People's Bank accounts and the clearing of the accounts for working hours and work performance.

It ensures compliance with the requirements on working conditions in the work areas for basic and luxury supply. It organises and coordinates the operation of Planned Businesses and Planned Enterprises. It supervises the Start-up Fund in cooperation with the Ministry of Finance and the Innovation Fund with the Ministry of Innovation. It ensures the beneficial effect of the laws on the establishment and operation of Innovation Enterprises and Experimental Enterprises. It ensures the operation of the People's Innovation Company[19] and the institutions for research and development in cooperation with the Ministry of Innovation.

18Ministry of Finance - 11 People's Bank
19Ministry of Innovation - 10 People's Innovation Company

2.5 Department for Economic Sectors of the Planned Economy

The Department for Economic Sectors of the Planned Economy coordinates the specialised locations and ensures the introduction or abolition of specialised areas. In voting with the Ministry of Infrastructure, it organises the building of the Social Villages and the transport connections between them. In cooperation with the Ministry of Integration, it ensures the operation of the houses for asylum seekers and coordinates the distribution of asylum seekers. In cooperation with the Note-issuing Bank for Planned Economy, it oversees the performance of the digital currency. It supervises Planned Economy joint-stock companies to see whether the requirements are beneficial or detrimental to overall economic development. In cooperation with the Ministry of Finance, it provides the necessary financial services, and with the Ministry of Labour, it provides insurance services. In cooperation with the ministries of labour, education and health, it organises agricultural supplies and runs the market gardens. It oversees foreign trade development and ensures that foreign trade balances are maintained. In cooperation with the Ministry of Foreign Affairs, it votes on continental social policy.

2.6 Department for State Services

The Department for State Services ensures that social welfare is adequately funded, that compensation payments are moved in from the affected Ministry of Economy and that the requirements of social legislation are met. It supervises the service delivery of the other ministries, ensures accounting and makes sure that tax revenues cover costs. It proposes changes to the corporate tax rate to the Minister for Planned Economy as appropriate. In cooperation with the Budget Committee, it ensures the distribution of profits from Planned Business and Planned Enterprise.

In cooperation with the Ministry of Infrastructure, it ensures the operation of the energy centres and the construction of real estate, transport routes and pipelines in the Social Villages. It operates the homes for children and the disabled in cooperation with the Ministry of Family Affairs, the Health Centre with the Ministry of Health, the Education Centre with the Ministry of Education, the Security Centre with the Ministries of Security, Justice and Finance, and the Town Hall with the Ministry of State Organisation. It operates the Leisure Centre as a Planned Business and provides technical advice and funding through the Ministries of Labour, Education, Family, Health and Infrastructure.

The Department for State Services coordinates education policy with the Ministries of Labour, Education and Digital, and the Ministries of Economy and Enterprises in all Ministries of Economy. It operates employment exchange services through the Social Villages in cooperation with the Ministry of Labour. It coordinates the cooperation between the Social Villagers and the Ministry of Media Affairs for the operation of the radio and TV channels. It operates the asylum houses in cooperation with the Ministry of Integration and coordinates the division into the Social Villages.

The Department for State Services operates them mobile Social Villages and coordinates their operation sites. In the event of a disaster, this department is responsible for organising the conversion of production in Planned Economy companies and, if necessary, in the other economic forms.

3 Tasks of the Ministry of Planned Economy

The task of the Ministry of Planned Economy is to organise the government of the Social Villages in the sense of dynamic media democracy. This gives Social Villagers the opportunity to participate to a greater or lesser extent in the government and shaping of enterprise policy. The Ministry of Planned Economy has the task of supporting the coexistence of the Social Villagers. On the one hand, this is done through digital applications in the Social Directory or with the Social Card and, on the other hand, through the possibilities for self-organisation in communities for living, working and organising leisure time.

The Ministry of Planned Economy regulates the right of residence in the Social Villages. Linked to this are requirements for voluntary or necessarily moving in, moving between economic forms, site selection, death and moving out. The Ministry of Planned Economy has the task to make the necessarily stay as short as possible for Social Villagers and as comfortable as possible for voluntary Social Villagers.

With its economic policy, the Ministry of Planned Economy fulfils the task of enabling a minimum level of prosperity, economic development in the interests of the population and sustainable growth through the alliance of all Social Villages. The ministry has a special role in the economic cycle with the other economic forms, especially the market economy, whose waste and unemployed are upgraded.

With its enterprise policy, the Ministry of Planned Economy pursues the task of democratically negotiating and coordinating the management, needs assessment, consumption, prices and the duty roster. In this way, the Ministry of Planned Economy ensures a balance of supply and demand for the benefit of the working and at the same time consuming population of the Social Villages. In order to provide revenues and property for the Social Villagers, the Ministry of Planned Economy regulates the use of people's property to generate private and municipal revenues.

With the work area of basic supply, the Ministry of Planned Economy fulfils the task of supporting the Social Villagers with essential goods and services. Social Villagers are responsible for providing goods and services through compulsory working hours in Planned Businesses and Planned Enterprises.

With the luxury supply work area, the Ministry of Planned Economy fulfils the task of enabling Social Villagers to do voluntary work for the production of desirable luxury goods, for setting up businesses or for research.

Through the economic sectors of Planned Economy, the Ministry provides for the independent production of all Social Villages' own needs. The Ministry of Planned Economy ensures the operation of Social Villages that specialise in large-scale industrial production in various sectors. Through the real estate sector, the ministry fulfils the task of ensuring that there is enough space for housing, working and living and that conflicting interest groups do not get in each other's way. Through the finance economy and currency policy, the ministry ensures a stable currency and value creation oriented towards rising living standards and more leisure time. With agriculture, the ministry fulfils the task of using the land of the Social Villages as optimally as possible for the production of renewable raw materials, food and medicine. With its foreign trade, the ministry protects Planned Economy from exploitation by other economic forms or the global economy, ensures a balanced foreign trade and enables new companies to enter the market.

The Ministry of Planned Economy's tax policy is designed to cover the expenses of the other ministries' services and to allow Social Villagers to share a part of their community revenues.

The task of the Planned Economy is to guarantee social rights through social welfare. The ministry ensures the necessary regularisation of social welfare funding.

The tasks of the other ministries in the Planned Economy are administration, security, health, rehabilitation, energy supply, support for the disabled, children, senior citizens and asylum seekers, as well as the placement of the unemployed and information.

In the event of a disaster, the Ministry of Planned Economy has the task of adequately supporting the population and the security forces, if necessary nationwide.

4 Social Village government[20]

The Ministry of Planned Economy pursues an economic policy that allows the economic form to exist autonomously. The other economic forms can trade conditionally with the Planned Economy, but have no say in how and with whom work is done. The autonomy of the Planned Economy can be limited by the Constitution and the Ministries of Labour and Health.

Social Villagers mainly administer themselves at the municipal level and form a municipal alliance of all Social Villages to support each other.[21] Compared to other municipalities, more services are offered and provided by the municipal community. The Social Villagers democratically decide which of them will provide which of these services, when and how. If the voting results between Social Villagers and the rest of

20 §130,2,3 Cultural protection areas and economic zones: BV Art.50
21 Ministry of State Organisation - 11.5.6 Cooperation between municipalities

the people differ, a decision is made in favour of the affected Social Villagers or a People's Committee has to be convened.

4.1 Social Villagers

Social Villagers are solidary and self-determined citizens who organise and coordinate their labour democratically. They use their labour power to support, amuse and educate each other as well as to research and invent new things together. They also house and support needy children, the elderly, the sick and the disabled within their means with state support in the form of skilled workers and equipment.

4.2 Politicians of the Planned Economy

For all circumstances that distinguish a Social Village from a municipality of the market economy, the Ministry of Planned Economy is responsible. For all other areas, the responsibility lies with the respective ministry. The responsible contact person for the Social Villagers is the deputy minister of the relevant ministry. The deputy minister for Planned Economy, elected by the Social Villagers, is responsible for the operation of the work areas for basic supply and luxury supply, as well as for the establishment and closure of Planned Businesses and Planned Enterprises. Responsibility for the living areas of housing, food, clothing and hygiene is the responsibility of one politician each, who is directly elected by the Social Villagers. As soon as the provision in one of the areas of life becomes deficient, the Social Villagers can force this politician to the committee through a veto quorum or dismiss him via the deselection quorum.[22] The same applies to the deputy ministers.

---

22 Ministry of State Organisation - 9.5.14 Veto quorum, 9.5.10 Deselection quorum, 9.6 Committee

4.3 Cabinet

The cabinet of a Social Village consists of the deputy ministers for Labour, Education, Digital, Family, Finance, Health, Infrastructure, Innovation, Integration, Justice, Media, Security, State Organisation and Planned Economy, as well as the politicians for Housing, Food, Clothing and Sanitation. The election of all posts is direct and new election takes place once a deselection quorum of 50% is reached. The cabinet determines the implementation of services and the fulfilment of needs assessment in its meetings. Social Villagers can move Cabinet meetings to committees through a 30% veto quorum. All cabinets of all Social Villages travel to the capital city of Planned Economy for a week each year and meet together before the annual needs assessment in all Social Villages. Exchanges of labour, goods, assets and responsibilities are negotiated and successful strategies are shared. All meetings are open to the public and are broadcast on the Social Villages' regional Citizen Television .[23]

4.4 Plenary assembly

To exchange ideas and vote, there is a plenary assembly every Sunday afternoon in the community hall or on the village square. Here, residents form discussion groups and draw up lists of speakers for suggestions, initiatives, arbitrations, duty roster dial-in, neighbourhood communication, basic supply and business start-ups. In small groups, the individual cases are discussed, a solution formulated and presented to the plenary assembly for voting. All ministries present their projects that affect the Social Village here, and the residents can decide whether they want to continue to be involved in the projects directly democratically or trigger the participation quorum. Constitutional rights and national law must not be broken in the process. Music and dance will take place during short breaks and afterwards.

---

23 Ministry of Media - 9.1 Regional Citizen Television

4.5 People's Computer

Every Social Villager has their People's Computer and a charging facility in their room. The People's Computer is more in demand than ever in Planned Economy. Social Villagers coordinate their life together on the noticeboard in the Town Hall, on the Town Hall Intranet Café and digitally in the Social Directory. People's Computers are compulsory at plenary assemblies to digitise voting so that Social Villagers who are not at the venue can also participate in the plenary assembly.

4.6 Social Directory

The Social Directory is a digital replica of the Social Village using satellite imagery. Residents are represented as coloured dots. By means of a sorting command, all dots can be assigned to activities. For example, all members of the swimming club are displayed or all those who are assigned to the duty roster in the canteen kitchen on Sunday evenings.

The view can be changed via a menu, from the satellite view to the network view for profiles and groups with their posts and comments. Here, all groups and profiles of the Social Village are displayed on the start page. All groups and profiles of all Social Villages can also be displayed via the extended view.

Every Social Villager joins with their profile from the Persons Directory. Every Social Village, state enterprises, unification, house and company has a profile in the Social Directory.

The Social Directory offers every unification of persons the possibility to present themselves to the public through a group. Residents can create closed groups in order to exchange information digitally. Groups can be open to all users, all Social Villages, all Social Villagers or closed so that only invitees can become members.

Through a function, all directories of all ministries can be limited to one's own or all Social Villages. For example, the Labour Directory only displays employers from the work area luxury supply of one's own Social Village.

Residents should be able to network easily through the Social

Directory to organise leisure activities together or form work groups to implement an entrepreneurial venture.

4.6.1 Simulation social world

The entire Planned Economy is mapped in a real-time computer game. The Ministry of Digital Affairs is responsible for programming and integration into the Social Directory. The algorithms synchronise all workloads of all enterprises for all offers with the demand of all Social Villagers. Similar to the game "Anno"[24] the satisfaction of the population is determined by the workload and the available supply. In the "strategy game" mode, decisions for the future can be simulated by digitally reducing or increasing the number of people and trading with other Social Villages or economic forms. The simulation is based on the latest data from all economic forms. Business founders can also use the game to simulate their prospects for success and sales markets.

In the "First Person Perspective" mode, Social Villagers can see their virtual Social Village and create an avatar. With the avatar they can interact with other avatars in the Social Village, similar to the game "Sims"[25] . Social Villagers can use it to meet each other in the digital or real world.

4.7 Social card

At the gate, all Social Villagers receive their Social Card when they move in. They can use it to log on to any device or building in the Social Village, thereby gaining admission or authorisation to use services in the Social Village. Each card has a passport photo, the holder's name, birthday and place of birth on the front and a magnetic strip and signature space on the back. Inside is a microchip.

The Social Card serves as a key card for doors in the Social Village, for using the centres and all services there, as well as a money card and time clock card.

___

24https://de.wikipedia.org/wiki/Anno_%28Spieleserie%29
25https://de.wikipedia.org/wiki/Die_Sims

All services provided by the Social Village, such as housing, food, health, hygiene, education, work and leisure, are charged to the card. The working hours of this month for the work area basic supply are booked on the card and the wages from the work area luxury supply are paid on it.

You can only pay with the Social Card in the Social Villages, but everywhere. The goods and services of the basic supply are only granted as long as all compulsory work has been done in the past month.

Services or goods that are subject to a fee can be purchased at the social market with the card. The deciding factor is whether the social card holder has enough money in their People's Bank account or working hours in their work benefit account. The money card function is not a credit card. The purchase is automatically refused if the balance on the People's Bank account is not sufficient.

When moving out, the social card must be handed in again. The working hours from the work area basic supply expire. Saved working hours from the work area luxury supply remain in the work benefit account at the People's Bank and can be spent by the former Social Villager in any Social Village during his or her lifetime. Saved money from the work area luxury supply is transferred in full to the People's Bank account.

4.7.1 Children's card

All children living in the Social Village also receive a Social Card, which is an extended child ID card[26] . The child benefit, the access entitlement to age-appropriate care facilities and the work benefit account are stored on the card.

4.7.2 Visitor card

Anyone wishing to visit the Social Village must hand in their identity card at the gate. As a replacement for the expulsion, visitors receive a visitor card at the gate. It contains the same data as the identity card and a cash card function.

26Ministry of Family Affairs - 8.3 Child ID Card

There is an ATM at the gate where visitors and residents can load money from their account onto the money card. All chargeable services must be paid for using the card before they can be consumed. If the amount loaded is not sufficient, you have to go back to the ATM at the gate and top up or forego consumption. For visitors, there is a 40% surcharge on all services in addition to the cost-covering amount. The prices are posted at the entrance to the centres and in the social market at the place where the goods are stored. There is no value added tax on money charged at the vending machine. It is included in the 40% mark-up, which is 20% higher than in the market economy. Half of the revenues go to the Ministry of Finance and the other half to the producer, who has to pay the Planned Economy's corporate tax rate on them.

Visitors can use the visitor card to open the doors to the centres and their hotel room, but not to the residences, businesses and companies. Only if working hours have to be completed, the corresponding doors are unlocked by the Social Service at the reception.

Before leaving the Social Village, the money can be withdrawn from the card here again. The card must be returned to the gate when leaving in order to get the identity card back.

4.8 Activity communities[27]

The self-organisation principle of an activity community applies to clubs, Experimental Enterprises and Innovation Enterprises. It states that the participants themselves should procure, acquire and execute the knowledge necessary for their project. The execution is done democratically by finding a group of volunteers who share a common interest in the project. The group elects a leader and organises regular meetings. It seeks as many volunteers as necessary who have sufficient knowledge to participate in the desired project.

In the meetings, all participants propose a procedure and content for the upcoming meetings. They all share their ideas about the project. A voting takes place on the upcoming

---

27 §229.4 Unemployment, old-age, survivors' and disability benefits: BV Art. 111

procedure. Until the next meeting, all participants investigate in the Knowledge Directory whether their approach is appropriate for this project. This is the phase of swarm intelligence. In the next meeting, the knowledge findings are shared. Voting takes place on whether the procedure should be changed. Either the project can now be carried out or knowledge recharges are necessary in stages in order to carry out the project with the appropriate procedures. Instructions for the necessary devices are available in the Knowledge Directory. The activity community can decide through its leader to collect fees from all members in order to be able to buy necessary goods. In the self-organisation principle, all services are provided by the participants. Exceptions confirm this rule, for example if a service provider's assignment is short, but his training is lengthy or his equipment is expensive.

Activity communities can organise their meetings via the Social Directory by setting up a corresponding group. They have access to the premises and equipment of the Social Village, provided they are not already occupied. There are waiting lists for this case. The Social Service is responsible for lending out premises and devices as well as for issuing resources.

4.8.1 Organisation of living together

Barracks become state welfare centres with communist and Marxist characteristics. Voluntary and needy citizens live here in Planned Economy structures with direct democratic decision-making processes for organising their life together. The standard of living is modest and ensures the residents a subsistence level of housing, food, clothing, hygiene and health. Luxury goods can be bought by the residents in community orders with quantity discounts in the market economy or produced by themselves. Residents can earn the money for this through gainful employment in Planned Economy companies, which receive payments in the national or international currency from their trade with the market economy. The Planned Economy companies cover their expenses with the revenues and distribute the remaining amount as wages to the employees. These wages form the foreign exchange reserves of the Planned Economy. The amount of foreign reserves determines the level of prosperity above the subsistence level. The Ministry of Planned Economy receives the business taxes of the Planned Economy companies as foreign reserves to purchase new technologies for the Social Villages.

4.8.1.1 Helpfulness

All nationals who are in need can ask for help at the Social Village gate or dial the social emergency number and be picked up for moving in to the Social Village. Desperate and lonely persons, regardless of age, are either further educated, employed, advised or find social contacts in the Social Village. In distress, everyone is allowed to stay at the Social Village Hotel until it can be clarified what the future help plan will be.
Social Villagers are basically encouraged to be helpful. This basic attitude becomes clear when moving in. The new neighbours have to help with moving in and explain life in the Social Village to their new neighbours. Anyone who needs support in any endeavour in the Social Village can ask all Social Villagers directly, publish their request in the Social Directory or call out at the weekly plenary assembly.

4.8.1.2 Peaceful and innovative togetherness

In the Social Villages, the residents live in a social village community. Everyone knows everyone else, or at least all neighbours and colleagues. A lively civil society is desired that looks out for each other in the sense that no one comes to unintended damage. Anyone who feels injustice should write it down immediately and report it to the next plenary assembly. The plenary assembly is in a position to adopt remedial measures, punitive measures or rules. Spying or malicious gossip are known from close-knit village communities. Many villagers therefore like to move to the anonymity of the city. Therefore, special communication rules apply in the Social

Village, because privacy is to be respected, but anonymity is a hindrance to social togetherness. Criticism should only be expressed together with a suggestion for improvement. Criticism may only be expressed to the person it concerns. Anyone who criticises residents in their absence in front of other residents, talks badly or spreads lies or assumptions will be punished.[28] In Planned Economy, residents are more dependent on each other than elsewhere. Disturbed social relations therefore have an immediate impact on productivity and lead to a higher workload for everyone.

4.8.2 House communities

Social Villages are structured similarly to "centre parks"[29], known from the tourism industry. Here, however, all services are paid for by the beneficiaries in working hours to receive all services in the Social Village. As in centre parks, Social Villages have different houses where children, couples, senior citizens, families and single persons live together. Depending on the age and life situation, suitable services are offered in the houses. These services are free of charge and based on the principle of self-organisation. There is a database of activities in the Knowledge Directory specifically for social village houses. Since all Social Villages are similarly equipped, premises and materials available in all Social Villages can be included in the offer. Purchases for which a fee is charged are consistently dispensed with in these offers.

In the houses, the residents elect a responsible person, the So-called Animator. They vote him out of office by a quorum of 60% of those affected. He looks for volunteers to lead and supervise an offer. The offer is primarily aimed at the house residents. Other Social Villagers may only be excluded if capacities are exhausted. The animator determines whether the capacities are exhausted. House residents have the right to report to the animator whether their capacities are exhausted or can be expanded again.

Animators receive credit for one working hour per week in the

---

28 Ministry of Justice - 8.16.5 Blasphemy
29 https://de.wikipedia.org/wiki/Center_Parcs

work area basic supply.

4.8.2.1 Animation in the houses

Animators lead different activities depending on the type of house. They download the appropriate instructions from the Knowledge Directory and organise the activities on a weekly basis. For example, in the children's house, games such as cops and robbers can be played. In the house for unmated persons, it's get-to-know-you games, and in the family house it's board games. In the home for the elderly, yoga exercises can be done together. In the house for couples, massage instructions can be implemented together.

4.8.3 Self-sufficiency

The Social Villages are designed to support themselves in the long term. In the introductory phase, the taxpayer supports the Social Villages. Most services by skilled workers and goods are imported from the market economy. Thereafter, all regular consumed goods and services of all Social Villagers are produced in Social Villages or done by skilled workers trained in the Social Village. All Social Villages are in the trade network and specialise in sectors. A balanced ratio of imports and exports is achieved. In the long run, an export surplus can be created by selling innovations on the world market. The Planned Economy can reliably absorb and hand over unemployed people from the market economy without endangering the basic supply. Humans who want to live in the Social Village on a voluntary basis can also be found.

Through the Social Directory, all Social Villagers can vote on their demand for goods and services. Their actual consumption is recorded by the Social Card and is used as a proposal in the upcoming needs assessment.

The Social Villagers administer themselves by electing leaders, moderators and animators and deselecting them by quorum. These elected persons ensure that the demand is matched by a suitable offer. The duty rosters to fulfil all offers are accessible via the Social Directory. For the work area of basic supply, Social Villagers elect responsible politicians and organise themselves into Planned Businesses and Planned Enterprises via the central digital duty roster. In the luxury supply work area, more Self-sufficiency is again required. Social Villagers voluntarily sign up for the duty roster for Experimental Enterprise, Innovation Enterprise, Planned Enterprise and People's Innovation Company.

4.9 Leisure

The Social Villagers organise their free time on a voluntary basis. A Social Village has many opportunities to spend free time with other humans through its recreational park and clubs. The ratio of work to free time depends on the needs assessment and the productivity of the workers. The working hours of the enterprises are set in such a way that basic supply is guaranteed around the clock and emergency services are available on holidays. The basic principle is that basic supply requires as little working time from each individual as possible. Behind this principle is Planned Economy's aim to give its residents as much free time as possible.

4.9.1 Clubs

In each Social Village there are clubs for young and old for nature, crafts, culture, exercise, homework and play. Examples of unifications would be scouts, craftsmen, artists, readers, handball players. Clubs in the vicinity of the Social Village can use the Social Village if at least 50% of the members are Social Villagers. If the Social Village is used, no membership fees may be charged for Social Villagers. The Social Village clubs maintain exchange programmes with other clubs.[30] The exchange is intended to promote contact with the outside world of the Social Village.

---

30 Ministry of Family Affairs - 9.6 Clubs

4.9.2 Neighbourhood

In the Social Village, one day a year is neighbourhood time. The neighbours of a house determine the day themselves. This day is a fixed holiday in the Social Village. All the people from the houses can go out into the street and talk, plan or celebrate with each other. This is to create opportunities to talk about problems with behaviour, distribution of tasks, worries or to strengthen the sense of community through, celebrations, dances, music or sports.

4.9.3 Open Day

Once a year there is an Open Day when persons are allowed to visit all the farms, centres and parts of the Planned Enterprise in Social Villages. All residents work on this day to test the operations under full load. All centre services are available to visitors on that day at a fixed price, including an overnight stay. Social Villagers are not subject to any caps on consumption on the day after. This tests desirable goods and maximum demand.

4.9.4 Church in the Social Village

In every Social Village with enough believers, all believers can build a church together. No matter which religion is practised, services take place in this church. For this purpose, there are various mobile furnishings in the building, such as altars, carpets or folding benches. The walls are white and in the middle of the room there are projectors that can project images of saints, symbols, scripture or colour plays on the walls. If there are not enough worshippers living in a Social Village, the community hall can be used by any religion for 2 hours a week.

5 Economic policy[31]

The Ministry of Planned Economy pursues an economic policy that is as self-sufficient as possible. Food and supplies are financed by compensatory payments as long as the Planned Economy cannot support itself because too many unemployed people from the Social Market Economy and Free Market Economy migrate or workers emigrate. Goods, services or work equipment are exchanged to support an even supply.

The division into two work areas makes it possible to permanently guarantee sufficient housing, food, hygiene and clothing as well as the possibility to generate additional revenues and to start or close companies without causing a breakdown of the supply system.

In the long term, the Planned Economy should generate economic growth through technical progress by increasing the number of innovations, ensure permanent full employment in the country and help to reduce the tax burden through profits.

5.1 Central economic policy

The Minister for Planned Economy is responsible for coordinating all Social Villages so that Planned Economy functions as stably as possible through the alliance of all Social Villages in the country. Stable functioning is considered to be ensured when all residents of the Social Villages are supported, no debts or tax money are necessary, but profits are generated from business start-ups.

The Minister of Planned Economy works with the other Ministers to provide their state services across the board in all Social Villages. He is supported by the Company Auditing Agency, which provides him with data on the quality and scope of services.

He works with the ministers of the market economy to link the economic cycles in such a way that the surplus economy gives its surpluses to the shortage economy and the shortage economy brings its innovations and skilled labour to the surplus economy.

31 §229,2,3,4 Unemployment, old-age, survivors' and disability pensions: BV Art. 111

The Minister of Planned Economy ensures equal rights and similar duties in all Social Villages. Compulsory work may vary slightly due to different workloads in the Social Villages. He is responsible for ensuring that all Social Villages can maintain their basic supply as independently as possible, sharing the workload among themselves.

The administration of the Planned Economy in the capital city administers the networking between the administrations of the Social Villages. In this way, the specialisation of the individual Social Villages in particular should lead to the fairest possible barter trade with all the goods that the Social Villagers have requested in the needs assessment.

The Procurement Office[32] is used to vote on what goods the ministries need and order them from Planned Enterprises in the Planned Economy. This includes the production of weapons for the Ministry of Security. Since the other ministries incur costs with their services in the Social Villages, supplies of goods or services can at least partially settle these costs through barter.

5.2 Regional economic policy[33]

The deputy ministers for Planned Economy are responsible for effective cooperation among Social Villagers in the Social Villages. They are the link between those entitled to vote in Planned Economy and the minister in the capital city for Planned Economy. They are responsible for the adequate service delivery of the centres in their Social Villages and sustainable growth.

The deputy ministers for Planned Economy inform the Social Villagers about the statistics of growth and demography in order to develop a strategy with them that meets the needs of as many residents as possible.

Each Social Village town hall is home to the administration of the Social Village. The town halls allocate as many jobs as possible in the work area of basic supply in order to have to

---

32 Ministry of Labour - 6 Procurement Office
33 §229.4 Unemployment, old-age, survivors' and disability benefits: BV Art. 111

finance their services through as little tax money as possible. The Social Service provides for the communal use of buildings and their equipment by allowing items and property to be lent out by Social Villagers.

5.3 Competition and structural policy

In Planned Economy, competition policy only exists to the extent that competition consists of securing the basic supply with the least possible expenditure of time in order to have more free time in which to have fun, realise ideas or earn money. These decisions are made by each person personally, but the joint voting happens automatically through a digitalisation that evaluates consumer behaviour and production methods and leads to a balanced relationship between supply and demand. Consumer policy is made by the Social Villagers themselves through needs assessment and influencing suppliers in the plenary assembly. Regional economic policy is pursued in the Social Villages by locating suitable or more specialised businesses in regions with resident skilled workers or few jobs. In regions of the country with few jobs, People's Innovation Companies can be established in addition to Social Villages.

Chambers of Industry and Commerce are replaced by the Social Village Cabinet, which works with the residents of all Social Villages under the direction of the Minister of Planned Economy. As companies and businesses in Planned Economy are democratically run, there are also directly elected managing directors.

Anyone who falsely accounts for working hours or favours certain persons is committing nepotism. Depending on the frequency and severity of the offence, additional working hours or detention may be imposed.[34]

---

34 Ministry of Justice - 8.16.3 Nepotism

5.4 Medium-sized business policy

Craftspersons and tradesmen are promoted by Planned Enterprises. Skilled craftspersons receive tools and building materials, orders and in-service training as journeymen. Craftspersons can request additional workers to assist them with work in the basic supply work area. Business support is provided by making rooms, equipment and tools freely available for developing innovations or testing business ideas. Innovation Enterprises receive money from the Innovation Fund and Experimental Enterprises receive money from the Start-up Fund. Liberal professions can offer their services in the Planned Economy if they live there themselves. The service economy of basic supply is offered in the supply centre, where trade in the form of the social market is also located. The Social Villagers determine the tourism policy and have to sacrifice free time for it in order to be able to pursue a special leisure activity. The plenary assemblies, after a committee, decide whether and how much work to put into the Leisure Centre and holiday areas in idyllically located Social Villages should be offered as part of basic supply or luxury supply.

5.5 Economic cycle

The Planned Economy is a scarcity economy because only as much is produced as has been ordered. The market economy is a surplus economy because as much is produced as could be sold. In a hybrid economic system, it is beneficial to create a circuit of surplus and scarcity to avoid wasting human and natural resources.

5.5.1 Recycling of goods

Social Villagers recycle the waste from the overproduction and abundance of the market economy. Bulky waste, old clothes, leftover food from supermarkets and canteens, depreciated machines from companies in the Social Market Economy and Free Market Economy, everything is collected by the Social Service. These leftovers are repaired, refurbished and used in the Social Village, or if no Social Villager needs them, they are sold on an online marketplace and sold into the market economy after deduction of business tax. This work is done by a Planned Enterprise and enables Social Villagers to earn money in the luxury supply work area. If the products are consumed in the Planned Economy, the workers earn working hours that they can exchange for benefits. If the products are sold into the market economies, the workers earn foreign exchange. The selling price for Social Villagers is based on the prevailing hourly wage, the labour time spent and the cost of materials and tools. Price reductions or Dutch auctions are possible in case of lack of demand.

Whether electrical appliances, furniture or clothes, everything can be bought at the social market. Customers from the Social Village pay the cost-covering price with their working hours from the luxury supply work area. Customers from the surrounding market economy may also shop there, but it is more expensive. A 40% surcharge is added to the cost-covering price. 20% goes to the Social Village as business tax and 20% as profit sharing to the Social Villagers who produce or provide services.

5.5.2 Upgrading the workforce

The circuit applies not only to goods but also to labour. In the market economy there is unemployment, in the Planned Economy full employment. As soon as the market economy produces the unemployed, the democratic Planned Economy saves the unemployed from inaction and being regulated by others. The Planned Economy offers opportunities for education and training as a qualified skilled worker as well as conducive conditions for business start-ups. In this way, the Planned Economy imports the unemployed from the market economy and exports skilled workers and companies. The Ministry of Planned Economy also operates the job bus for employment exchange and organises job fairs and employer visits.

5.6 Economic development

The overall economic development of Planned Economy is recorded through analyses by the economic auditors so that projections are possible through the Algoracle[35]. The Company Auditing Agency collects all the necessary data via the intranet. The Ministry of Digital Affairs is responsible for providing the data from all directories and for programming the algorithms and programmes. The Social Directory represents the totality of all labour, labour tools, inputs, Food and living spaces available in the Planned Economy. This makes it easier for the administration and the population to observe, provides an overview, and facilitates exchange between the Social Villages. Individual production or living methods can be tested in small, localised pilot projects, So-called real laboratories. The Minister for Planned Economy regularly informs all Social Villagers about economic developments in the regional news of the Social Villages. All the above administrative activities can be negotiated by the informed Social Villagers with the Minister in a committee once the veto quorum of 30% is met.

5.7 Sustainable growth

Sustainable growth means that all raw materials have sufficient time to grow back. In agriculture, this is done through perennial, steadily growing crops and livestock herds. Sustainable growth in the economy takes place through the steady production of newer machines and materials with greater benefits or lower costs. The focus of economic and structural policy research is on biotechnology in order to be able to use renewable raw materials. Sustainable growth also requires healthy demographics. The population should be as balanced as possible in all age groups. A birth rate of two children per woman ensures that the population remains constant so that jobs can be filled and the standard of living can rise. A growth in the population results in higher turnover, but no increase in living standards.

For sustainable growth, an overcapacity of 10% is kept in the

---

35 Ministry of Digital Affairs - 15.3 Algoracle

Social Villages. As soon as the overcapacity is below 10% and above 5% for more than one year, the need for action arises for the Minister of Planned Economy.

5.7.1 Economic fluctuations[36]

The Ministry of Planned Economy provides management of the available amount of working hours. Because the number of Social Villagers fluctuates, the basic supply must be flexible to accommodate different numbers of residents. This is achieved by keeping 10% overcapacity in all living and working places. If the overcapacity is called up, the regular residents first work overtime, and as soon as the newcomers have been trained, they work minus hours. Incomers use vacant rooms or stored machinery. The Ministry of Planned Economy monitors and estimates how capacity utilisation will behave in the future. If the utilisation of overcapacity rises permanently above 5%, construction measures are initiated. If, on the other hand, capacity utilisation falls, machines, rooms and buildings are shut down or put into storage. Deconstruction does not take place. If too few Social Villagers have to take on too much work in the Social Village, so that their workload is 15% above normal, entire Social Villages are abandoned and their buildings rented out and residents relocated. Rented Social Villages must remain intact so that they can be used again in the Planned Economy in the event of a downturn. The sale of real estate or goods after the dissolution of a Social Village is only permitted with the consent of the people, as it is the property of the people. Because Social Villages are used as barracks in the event of war, they may not be sold, but only rented out when empty.

5.7.2 Shrink

As soon as the number of Social Villagers falls below a critical mass, Self-sufficiency can no longer be guaranteed because not all basic supply positions can be filled. In this case, Social

---

36§227,1,2 Rental business: BV Art. 109

Villages can cease operations and be released for rent. All rental contracts contain a termination clause in case social village operations have to be resumed or used as barracks in case of war.

5.7.3 Grow

A growing population of Planned Economy through more volunteers or indigents or a birth rate above two, forces the Ministry of Planned Economy to take over land. The state administration administers sufficient land. The aim is to avoid having to expropriate, resettle and compensate local residents. Company sites are obliged to relocate, but they must not suffer any loss of production. This is ensured by completing the new location before closing the old one.

5.8 New construction of a Social Village[37]

When a Social Village grows, the deputy reports this to the Minister for Planned Economy. He decides on relocations to shrinking Social Villages or those with free capacity. If 90% of the capacity limits are reached, another Social Village is built. The Minister for Planned Economy convenes committees in the designated areas and negotiates with residents to convert the area into a Social Village. Residents are all citizens living within a 10km radius of the possible Social Village. In the following voting, the people decide on the conversion. The result shows, firstly, whether a conversion may take place. For this purpose, the votes of the people are evaluated. Secondly, the result shows where more residents are in favour of conversion. The Social Village is created where most residents have voted for a conversion.

---

[37]§229.3 Unemployment, old-age, survivors' and disability benefits: BV Art. 111

6 Switching between economic forms

Switching between economic forms is connected with numerous requirements in the Planned Economy. The entrance of persons can be voluntary or necessarily, whereby the necessarily entrance is connected to the receipt of social benefits. The entrance of companies depends on whether they can meet a need of the Social Villagers. For the audit of changing companies, the Company Auditing Agency conducts special audits.[38] The Ministry of Finance is responsible for changing business tax.[39] For persons and companies, entry fees amount to the cost of moving and expanding capacity in the Social Village.

Exit is possible for persons as soon as all compulsory work has been done or paid for. Withdrawal fees apply if payments or work services are outstanding and if items of the Planned Economy are to be bought off and taken away. For enterprises, exit is only possible if their services are no longer needed or the company is to be closed. Innovation Enterprises and Experimental Enterprises can exit the Planned Economy as soon as they can cover the market entry costs.

Only the export of surplus goods and services is possible. This applies to persons and companies. For persons, sufficient foreign exchange reserves are necessary for the import of goods and services. For companies, there must also be a balanced foreign trade account if the import is regular and in large quantities.

6.1 Entrance to the Planned Economy[40]

The motivation to move into a Social Village can be the Planned Economy democratic work and village community, social need or unemployment. Only the first motivation is voluntary, the last two motivations are not voluntary but necessarily. Citizens considering a move to Planned Economy

---

38 Ministry of Labour - 10.2.2 Changing companies
39 Ministry of Finance - 5.2.7 Business taxes in the economic forms
40 §43 Social rights: KV Art.29, §229,2,3 Unemployment, old age, survivors and disability benefits: BV Art. 111, §230,2a Social Security, §186,2 Peaceful separation

can have this future living situation simulated in the Algoracle.[41]

All nationals can voluntarily move in and out of a Social Village or receive outpatient services. They are supervised and supported by the Social Service at all times. The Planned Economy provides social services as a social insurance for the citizens in the country, guaranteeing social rights. Citizens have the right to use these benefits, but not the obligation. All nationals and children are entitled to them. Special assistance is provided for the domestic unemployed, impoverished pensioners in need of care, victims of serious crimes, survivors and the disabled. Planned Economy residents provide this service in cooperation with the responsible ministries and receive taxpayers' money if necessary.

Whether foreigners, apart from asylum seekers, can be accepted in the Social Village depends on the budgetary situation of the Planned Economy. If the Planned Economy is dependent on tax money, social welfare for foreigners is not possible at all. If the Planned Economy has surpluses, the Social Villagers can vote to allow foreigners to receive assistance as long as surpluses continue to be generated. In the course of this, they can also decide on the influx of voluntary foreigners. The Social Villagers then democratically determine a quota of foreigners that must never jeopardise the basic supply.[42] Foreigners from Continental Union member states receive a residence permit in the Planned Economy, provided that the Planned Economy social systems have been unified. The Ministry of Planned Economy with its Continental Union social policy is responsible for this. In the long term, the exclusion of foreigners by the united states of the world will cease.

6.1.1 Voluntary moving in

Those who voluntarily move into the Social Village must pay the Social Service for transport or carry it out themselves. If a Social Village has reached its capacity limit, it is either necessary to choose another Social Village or wait until a place

---

41 Ministry of Digital Affairs - 15.3 Algoracle
42 Ministry of Integration - 7.4 Quota of foreigners

becomes available or the Social Village is expanded. Volunteers can help with the expansion by donating money and goods or by participating in the expansion work.

6.1.2 Moving in necessarily[43]

Humans who do not move into the Social Villages voluntarily always have the option of leaving the Social Village again and are not obliged to remain there. Persons who are unemployed, over-indebted, disabled, in pension or in special circumstances are considered necessarily.

Because the market economies have not been able to alleviate this need, they must provide compensation payments that pay for the professionals who become necessary to support those affected. Persons who move into Planned Economy out of need and can no longer lead their lives independently must state the exact reason. Depending on whether it is health or economic conditions, or help in special life situations, decides whether the Social Market Economy or Free Market Economy has to make compensation payments or not.

6.1.2.1 Unemployment

Unemployment means not being able to earn an income or sufficient income because there are no jobs to be found in the labour markets of the Social Market Economy and Free Market Economy. The unemployed are continuously reported as seeking in the Labour Directory. As soon as a job is advertised in the selected radius, the unemployed person receives a news item and can apply himself or automatically.

The unemployed choose an educational qualification of their choice for which there are currently vacancies in sectors of their choice. In the educational institutions, start-up seminars are held for all sectors, where unemployed people can get together to set up an Experimental Enterprise or an Innovation Enterprise.

During the further education leading to the desired degree,

43§229,2,4 Unemployment, old-age, survivors' and disability benefits: BV Art. 111

internships in companies in the chosen industry are to be undertaken during the holidays. For this purpose, the Social Service provides shuttle transport or a mobile home. The remuneration for an internship is first spent on the costs of the commute. As soon as in-service training is possible, the same procedure applies. As soon as sufficient income is earned in the market economy, moving out must take place.

6.1.2.2 Over-indebtedness

Those who can no longer pay their debts must file for private insolvency and can move into a Social Village. The debts are considered written off after 5 years of living in the Planned Economy. Any assets and income of over-indebted people are invested in a fund. After 5 years, the creditors get their debts back, remaining money is given to the over-indebted person, missing money is considered a loss for the creditors.
Anyone who owns an over-indebted company must file for insolvency and report for unemployment. The assets from a corporate insolvency are handled in the same way as in a private insolvency.

6.1.2.3 Special life situations

Special life situations can enter, for example, when addiction, serious acts of violence suffered, death or separation from relatives result in loss of income or psychological loss of control. Those who move into the Social Village because they are lonely and desperate are allowed to stay in the Social Village Hotel immediately and receive psychological care in the Health Centre and practical life advice from the Social Service within one week. Here, the affected citizen can also find out whether social village life would be helpful for him or whether another economic form or a cultural protection area would be more in line with his preferences for the care of social ties. Those who decide to live in the Social Village plan their moving in and stay with the Social Service.

6.1.2.4 Disability

Those who are mentally or physically disabled, unable to support themselves and work in the market economy are supported in the house for disabled people. Depending on the type of disability, it is made possible for the humans to participate in the duty roster at appropriate places. Workshops for disabled humans are set up accordingly. The rule of compulsory work in the work area of basic supply only applies as far as the degree of disability allows. Suitable work is reserved in the duty roster for this disabled person and cannot be democratically distributed among the Social Villagers.

Care volunteers or relatives of disabled people can move into the house for disabled people. They must take on at least the working hours in the work area basic supply and can pursue gainful employment outside or within the Social Village. The care hours for a disabled person are counted towards the working hours in the basic supply work area, depending on the degree of disability.

The degree of disability is determined at the health centre by an assessment according to the law on severe disabilities. If there are treatment methods that reduce or eliminate the disability, they are carried out. In the case of a reduction, it is decisive that the degree of disability decreases to such an extent and that at least one working hour can be saved in daily care. It is also decisive whether the treatment makes more work in the work area of basic supply or luxury supply possible, or even makes it possible to enter the market economy. Disabled people who establish a working life in the market economy receive integration support in the form of commuting and a move by the Social Service and implementation support by an advisor from the Company Auditing Agency for 6 months or during the trial period. The houses for disabled people ensure the implementation of the United Nations Convention on the Rights of Persons with Disabilities in the Planned Economy.[44]

---

44 https://www.behindertenbeauftragte.de/SharedDocs/Publikationen/ UN_Konvention_deutsch.pdf?__blob=publicationFile&v=2

6.1.2.5 Pension[45]

Those who have not made sufficient private pension provision to be able to live on the pension from the market economy can live in the Planned Economy. Those who have reached retirement age move into the senior citizens' house and are entitled to basic supply, the So-called basic pension. In the senior house, younger senior citizens care for older senior citizens as part of their compulsory working hours. Pensioners also have compulsory working hours in Planned Economy, until they die. Depending on the impairment, work is reserved in the duty roster for impaired senior citizens. Which physical or mental ailments are present is determined at the health centre by a medical certificate. The health auditors of the Company Auditing Agency[46] categorise work that can no longer be done with certain ailments.

Those who have a pension provision, but it is not enough to live on, continue to receive it, but from now on they have to pay tax on it at the Planned Economy's corporate tax rate. The remaining amount can be used to claim additional benefits or to buy goods and services in the social market. In the case of full inpatient care, without the possibility to perform compulsory working hours, the entire pension amount is transferred to the Social Village. The Social Village bears the costs of the funeral and the Social Service carries it out.

In order to enable impoverished pensioners to move out of the Planned Economy, they can participate in business start-ups in order to receive sufficient income to live in the market economy if they are successful. Impoverished pensioners are also free to move to a Barter Economy Zone or commit suicide at any time.

6.1.2.6 Social commuters

Social commuters receive outpatient social benefits and have to pay fees or work hours. As a social commuter, one can only receive certain social benefits, namely education, health and

---

45§230.2d Social Security: BV Art. 112
46Ministry of Labour - 20.7.2 Health auditor

business start-ups. One receives a social card on which benefits for education, health and business start-ups can be paid for with working hours, but all other benefits must be paid for in a market economy currency. If social commuters overload the Planned Economy, the ministries of the market economy have to make compensatory payments to increase capacity.

If the commute to work is no more than 10 kilometres, a bicycle is provided; beyond that, state transport can be used free of charge. If social commuters cannot travel by state transport, they are picked up and brought back by the Social Service in a car. This driving service can also be paid for with working hours.

6.2 Site selection

An algorithm in the digital administration[47] decides which Social Village is the most suitable for a citizen in need. It accesses all occupancy figures of the Social Villages, takes into account all personal data from the directories of the intranet, such as age, living situation, educational qualifications and working situation of the residents. In this way, vacancies in surrounding Social Villages are found that are available in the short, medium or long term. The Social Service search mask is also accessible to all other Social Directory users. Although the algorithm accesses all data of all citizens, it never displays them individually. Every citizen who makes a search query receives various proposals from the algorithm. The user can see which of his own personal data the algorithm has referred to. Now, in this view, one can give more or less weight to some personal data. There are sliders from 0 to 100 %. You can also select keywords that are important or unimportant to you. The algorithm is there to ask the crucial questions about which Social Village can best help a person. It is crucial to know which professional qualifications, experiences and interests can be used as strengths and which ailments, hardships or habits could be avoided, trained away or treated as weaknesses. This questionnaire can be completed from the People's Computer at home or with the help of the Social Service staff.

47 Ministry of Digital Affairs - 5 Digital Administration

If you choose a particular Social Village because of a training course, course of study, sector orientation or because of certain companies or enterprises, you will be given preference for accommodation there. By default, Social Villages are selected that are as close as possible to the old place of residence, if this is desired, and places are available. Those who have expertise through degrees can choose among the Social Villages where there is a shortage of these professionals. If one has had to move further away from one's old place of residence or to a Social Village other than the one desired, but wants to return as soon as possible, one may sign up on a list. If places become available there, it is the turn of those who have been on the list the longest so far.

If there are enough persons on the list for a new house, a new house is built in the Social Village. When the capacity of the kitchen, laundry or all other institutions is exhausted, one more floor is added to the centres. After three floors, more space has to be released for the Social Village.

6.3 Move

People in need of help who have reported to the Social Emergency Service are referred to the nearest Social Village during the initial counselling. The Social Emergency Call has cars at its disposal. Individuals or families are picked up after their emergency call and taken to the nearest social village hotel, unaccompanied minors to the children's home. After the counselling week, the persons are brought back home. If the persons decide to move into the Social Village, at least two new neighbours and Social Service furniture movers drive a truck to the persons' homes and help load the vehicles. The same procedure is used by persons who want to move into the Planned Economy on a voluntary basis. However, they make an appointment when there is enough space in the social village hotel and pay for this stay and the truck transport.

6.3.1 Personal move

The Social Service takes care of loading and transporting persons and objects. The new neighbours help with unloading into the new flat in the Social Village. Neighbours receive one working hour in the work area basic supply to help their new neighbours moving in.
Those who want to store furniture or large items that do not fit in their own cellar have to pay a monthly fee. Those who want to store their furniture or other items as common property, so that any Social Villager can lend them out, do not have to pay anything.

6.3.2 Financial move[48]

Those voluntarily moving into the Planned Economy must have closed all other private and business bank accounts and transferred the assets to the People's Bank Private and Corporate Account within 7 days of moving in. A one-time tax of 40% must be paid on these assets. Sums of money invested in People's Bank accounts or People's Stock Exchange accounts are exempt from this. Investing money via the People's Stock Exchange is still possible, but the Planned Economy corporate tax rate on financial income applies.
Those who necessarily move into the Planned Economy can preserve assets if possible. A distinction is made between assets that are preserved because they are able to generate profits and assets that must be sold in order to deposit the proceeds into the wealthy person's People's Bank account. Advice is given at the People's Bank branch in the Social Village. The advice is always given against the background that assets such as real estate, companies or things that serve to create value do not have to be sold. The existing assets in the market economy are to be preserved so that moving out of the Planned Economy is easier.
For example, someone loses his job but lives in a condominium. He can no longer pay the costs of the condominium. He can then move into the Social Village and rent out his

---

48 §218.6 State Bank, §227.3 Rental business

condominium. From the rental, he now has to pay the Planned Economy business tax rate. He can deposit the remaining proceeds in his People's Bank account to finance the cost of the flat and pay for the storage of his furniture in the Social Village. As soon as he has found a job, he can move back into his condominium with his furniture.

6.3.3 Move of entrepreneurs and companies[49]

Those who necessarily move into Planned Economy and own companies can continue to operate them and must continue to comply with the regulations of the respective Ministry of Economy. However, all corporate profits are subject to the Planned Economy tax rate. The responsible Ministry of Economy receives the regular corporate tax rate and the Ministry of Planned Economy receives the difference, up to the Planned Economy tax rate. Those entrepreneurs who lived in the Planned Economy for more than 5 years must transfer these companies to the Social Market Economy and follow the requirements for voluntary residents.

Those who voluntarily move into the Planned Economy and own companies must continue them in the Social Market Economy. The corporate tax rate is that of the Planned Economy. The tax rate of the Social Market Economy is paid to the Ministry of Social Market Economy. The remainder is remitted to the Ministry of Planned Economy up to the tax rate of the Planned Economy. The companies can remain in their traditional location and must meet the standards of the Social Market Economy. The employees are involved in a direct democratic way in the sustainable management of the company. Social Villagers are preferred over other applicants in job advertisements of these companies.

Those who own companies can also transfer them to Planned Economy, provided the company can contribute to basic supply or luxury supply. Depending on the size of the company, it may move into one or more Social Villages or remain at the location. If a company is to remain at the location, it must be close enough to a Social Village to allow

---

49 §150,1,3b,4 Business taxes

commuting of workers by Social Service vehicles or bicycle. If the company is large enough, a Social Village can also be built at the company's location. The company bears the costs for the necessary construction work, a shuttle service or the move. The Ministry of Planned Economy can make an advance payment and companies make a corresponding subsequent instalment payment through their revenues and also pay a 10% profit surcharge. The Social Villagers affected have to agree to the advance payments by a majority, as they are made from the Social Village's savings.

6.3.4 Trial period

A trial period of 4 weeks applies to living space and workplaces. During this time, neighbours or colleagues can get to know each other. At the end of the trial period, secret voting takes place to see if you fit together. The results are announced in private between the two parties. Those who do not wish to do so must write down or record their justification. This is to avoid that two Social Villagers who have rejected each other meet in the future and a silent and uneasy feeling arises in both.
Those who do not pass the trial period must move to a neighbouring flat or change to another job. The trial period can be failed a maximum of 2 times. The third time is followed by a negotiation before the Social Village's Negotiator's Court. It can provide integration assistance for the repeatedly rejected person or propose living as a hermit in the Barter Economy. After that, there is no trial period. Other Social Villagers are notified of this in the duty roster.

6.4 Illegal immigrants

Anyone who does not enter or leave the Social Village through the gate is liable to prosecution. Those who enter the Social Village receive either a Social Card or a Visitor Card and have to hand in their identity card in return. As soon as one leaves the Social Village, the card has to be returned and one gets one's identity card back. Anyone who does not do this is liable to prosecution. Anyone who stays in the Social Village longer than the specified time is liable to prosecution and must be placed in the detention cell in the security centre for the duration of the time overrun. Anyone who has been in the Social Village illegally for more than a week is liable to detention for the same period.

Illegal immigrants are reported by Social Villagers and detected with surveillance cameras or security guards. The entrances and exits of the centres and residences are equipped with card readers and cameras for facial recognition. An algorithm detects persons who are not entitled to admission because they are not registered at the gate or their period of stay has elapsed.

6.5 Death

From the age of 80, life-sustaining measures are no longer performed at the health centre. Suicide can also be requested at the health centre. After the psychological advice and notary appointments, suicide is facilitated in a room of the health centre by means of a poison potion.

Anyone who dies in the Social Village and has no money for burial in a cemetery gets an urn burial free of charge in the workers' tower of each Social Village. The tower replaces the cemetery and is built in such a way that it can grow up to 50 metres into the sky by always adding another floor if needed. A staircase with railings winds around the tower and leads up to the balconies. On the inside of the balconies are the compartments for the urns with plaques on the doors with names and dates of birth and death. At the top is a viewing platform. The floors with the balconies and the viewing platform can also be reached via an interior lift.

6.6 Exit from the Planned Economy

Anyone who wants to move out of the Social Village can do so independently at any time. To do so, the working hours account must be balanced. Upon exit, services may be subject to fees. These exit fees are calculated by a programme in the Social Directory. It shows the user which costs he or she can save through his or her own contribution.

For the exit, the working hours account must not be in the minus. If it is, the hours must be worked off or paid in the currency of the Social Market Economy. For moving out, either the Social Service can be booked for a fee or the transport is done on one's own. Items belonging to the Planned Economy can either be bought or they have to be returned. This is decided by the Social Service after balancing the stock. All stored items must either be taken away, given away or disposed of with costs. The neighbours will again receive compulsory working hours for helping with the moving out.

Anyone who came to the Social Village as an unemployed person and found a job in the market economy or started a company in the Planned Economy that became successful in the market economy must pay fees for the move to the Social Service, unless they can make the move themselves. Companies moving out of the Social Village into the market economy must make a takeover offer to their workforce. Operating resources that are to be taken with them can be purchased if the Social Service can register sufficient stocks.

6.7 Foreign exchange

All revenues of market economy currencies are considered foreign exchange. Foreign exchange can therefore be received in the currency of the Social Market Economy, Free Market Economy or a foreign currency with an exchange rate. The recipients of foreign exchange are the exporting companies of the Planned Economy. These companies pay the Planned Economy's corporate tax rate and thus part of the foreign exchange to the Ministry of Planned Economy. The Ministry of Planned Economy also receives foreign exchange from the influx of wealthy voluntary persons from the market economy who pay the Planned Economy tax rate on their assets and existing companies in the market economy. The amount of foreign exchange reserves available to the Ministry of Planned Economy, decides the maximum amount of goods and services that may be imported from the market economy in the coming year.

Planned Businesses and Planned Enterprises make their revenues from foreign exchange available to the residents of their Social Village, who decide on them together in the needs assessment and budget committee. Companies in the work area of luxury supply pay their employees a share of the foreign currency they earn. This means that employees and not only entrepreneurs have the opportunity to earn foreign currency. Social Villagers can use the foreign exchange they earn for consumption at the Social Market or savings at People's Bank. The companies can use their foreign currency to buy goods and services for their production or invest in innovations.

6.8 Import and export of goods and services

Import of goods and services from the market economy is only possible if the persons or companies have sufficient foreign exchange and the products are not available in the Planned Economy. Import from the Barter Economy is only possible if the counterpart can be provided by surplus goods and services. The Social Market is responsible for importing goods and services in each Social Village. It receives orders from the buyers' associations of Social Villagers and companies in the luxury supply work area.

All buyer associations decide in a voting for a product of their choice and buy it in a low-cost collective order on the world market. The importer is the Ministry of Planned Economy. There is a proviso that the Planned Economy exports enough so that there is no foreign trade deficit. Trade deficits with another domestic economic form are allowed as long as they are offset by surpluses in another economic form. Imports are replaced by services from Planned Enterprises if there is sufficient demand.

The export of goods and services is regulated differently for Planned Economy companies. Planned Businesses from the basic supply work area are only allowed to sell surplus production to the Social Market Economy. Planned Enterprises may independently export their goods and services to the market economy as long as the demand of the Planned Economy is met. There are no restrictions on exports for People's Innovation Company, Experimental Enterprise and Innovation Enterprise, as they are expected to earn maximum profits, pay business taxes and, if successful, leave the Planned Economy and pay foreign exchange into one of the funds on an ongoing basis.

6.8.1 Export of raw materials

Only disaster management can initiate the export of finite raw materials of basic supply to other economic forms. Raw materials that are not finite but perishable may be exported to all economic forms as long as the needs of all Social Villages are met. The raw material areas of the Planned Economy are sized to support all Social Villages at full capacity. The planned vacancy rate of 10% means that capacities are only exhausted at extraordinary peak times.

6.8.2 Buyers from the market economy

Purchases by citizens of the market economy are possible as long as this does not cause a shortage. Should a shortage occur, the service cannot be provided to shoppers. Social Villagers are supported preferentially. To enable shoppers to change money, there is a vending machine in each Social Village where shoppers can deposit their currency. The amount is then exchanged into Planned Economy's digital currency and credited to the visitor's card. This incurs 20% value added tax. The remaining amount has to be exchanged back when leaving the Social Village or is forfeited.

7 Enterprise policy[50]

The Ministry of Planned Economy regulates the principles of business management and ensures appropriate trade and craft laws in the work areas. The Planned Economy is divided into the work areas for basic supply and luxury supply. Within the work areas, there are specialisations in various economic sectors, mainly sorted by industry. There are six types of enterprises in the Planned Economy, namely State Enterprises[51] , Planned Enterprises, Experimental Enterprises, Innovation Enterprises and People's Innovation Company. State enterprises and Planned Businesses are exclusively active in basic supply. Planned Enterprises and Experimental Enterprises are active in basic supply and luxury supply. Innovation Enterprises and People's Innovation Companies are active in luxury supply.
An independent enterprise policy takes place within the work areas. All requirements and possibilities that apply to all companies in Planned Economy are listed below.

7.1 Democratic corporate governance

In companies, such as industry, commerce and craftspersons, operational decisions are found in a similar way as in state politics. Employees and customers represent affected citizens and elected superiors represent responsible politicians. The managing director of a company corresponds to an elected minister. The governed territory here is limited to the company premises and the niche in the market. There are parties for the individual company areas, such as human resources or accounting. Employees and customers can be members of several parties, inform themselves about the work areas and lobby for improvements.
The leader of a team or an entire company must always be elected by the employees. In the case of division of labour or part-time work, several leaders are elected accordingly. There shall be deselection by quorum, nomination from among the staff, presentation of the programmes with plans and morale in committees, and democratic conduct of elections and voting.

50§228,1b,1d,6 Labour: BV Art. 110, KV Art.39
51Ministry of Labour - 4 State enterprises

Elected superiors ensure the smooth functioning of the divisions and take up proposals from the party. If the superior does not take up the improvements, dissatisfied people can cast their vote for the new election of his post in the deselection quorum. Superiors and employees meet regularly in company committees to make deciders. This procedure can be used by small teams as well as the whole company.

7.2 Occupational health and safety protection of all work areas[52]

The Planned Economy is guided by the laws on occupational health and safety that apply in the Social Market Economy. However, employees can vote together for improvements, which then only apply in their company. Workplaces must be safe, must not endanger the health of employees and must not pollute the environment. Environmental pollution is only permissible if it can be disposed of without leaving residues and thus be environmentally neutral. Disposal costs must be included in the price. Employees may report unfair, unsafe or backward workplaces and goods or services hazardous to humans and the environment anonymously or in person in the Company Auditing Agency's annual audit.
Every business, every company and all workers are committed to democratic co-determination and compliance with the laws on occupational health and safety.

7.3 Needs assessment

In the needs assessment, available working hours are distributed among the companies in the work area basic supply and luxury supply. The annual needs assessment takes a maximum of one week and takes place digitally in the Social Directory. All Social Villagers are supposed to weigh up how much they consume and work or do without and have more free time. Therefore, several voting rounds are necessary.

---

52 §190,8 Environmental protection, §228,1a,1b Labour: BV Art. 110

7.3.1 Vote on demand

First, a vote on demand is held for goods and services. Everyone creates their shopping basket according to their own wishes. As soon as sufficient data is available, the person voting is shown how his or her consumption has been in the past year and month. The citizens of all Social Villages select quantities they would like to consume daily, weekly, monthly or at least once from a list of products and services. The citizens can add items to the list themselves during the vote on demand. The computer programme recognises similar entries and sorts them into the same category. An algorithm calculates whether this demand can be met. It shows how many hours each Social Villager would have to work or how much space would be needed. It also includes personal data, such as qualifications, age or health status of all Social Villagers. It also shows who would have to do without how much in order to distribute all the products demanded given capacities. This is used to calculate the amount of demand.

7.3.2 Vote on supply

After the vote on demand, the workload of working hours in the two work areas is calculated. Based on this result, the Social Villagers can now decide whether they want to work as much or less. They enter their desired number of working hours in both work areas. This is used to calculate the amount of work available. As soon as sufficient data is available, the person voting is shown how much work they have done in the past year and month. After the vote on supply, it is calculated how many and which goods and services are offered per capita. The algorithm calculates the probable yields of all yield areas and farms. It takes into account the possible weather and economic scenarios for a year and which plants or animals are most likely to survive in them. The electricity yields from wind and sun also flow into these forecasts. These forecasts form the available supply.

7.3.3 Vote on balance

Social Villagers vote several times in a row and can adjust their own demand according to the results of the votes. They can change their available working time for each work area individually and adjust their consumption quantities of goods and services. In the vote on balance, one can newly apply both previous voting options, but this time simultaneously. Through the algorithm, one can see how long one has to work to obtain the desired goods and services. The voting data is used to calculate a mean value that is presented to the Social Villagers for voting. Usually this mean is either the median or the average. If the mean does not receive a majority, the process is repeated and negotiated in a committee of the Ministry of Planned Economy.

7.3.4 Algorithm management

Manual needs assessment is time-consuming and, at once a year, so infrequent that it can cause shortages or surpluses because the quantities would then be fixed for a year. Needs assessment, however, is an important opportunity for residents to negotiate with each other what an algorithm otherwise does virtually throughout the year. The algorithm's activity is represented in the Social Directory as a virtual simulation.
Through the annual manual needs assessment, the algorithm receives its necessary data and the basic settings that will be used in the coming year. Through the voting on demand, supply and equilibrium, the algorithm has learnt the personal maximum work willingness and consumption expectation of all residents and how much each individual deviates from their maximum demand in order to achieve equilibrium. This gives the algorithm the data it needs to determine the elasticity of demand and supply.
Citizens can adjust the code of the algorithm in a collective voting. Individual adjustments during the year can be made by a veto quorum of 30% of all Social Villagers.

7.3.5 Digital management of the supply volume

The algorithm continuously calculates all data in real time throughout the year and updates its forecasts based on the current situation. It uses the data of all time clocks, cash registers and doors in the Social Villages as well as the audit results of the Company Auditing Agency for this purpose. The demand is automatically forwarded to the appropriate producers and the duty roster is automatically adjusted. If manual changes are to be made to the duty roster, all affected colleagues vote together and change the digital duty roster accordingly. The condition is that the quantity offered remains the same.

Should a supply deviation of more than 10% occur, a needs assessment is triggered. Demand may be shifted down, up or to substitute goods or services, depending on the situation. Overproduction may be consumed by Social Villagers or sold in the market economy. This is decided at a plenary assembly.

7.4 Consumption

Consumption of goods and services is possible in the centres or the social market. There are card readers at all cash registers, which are used to charge for the goods. Those who want to consume more than their basket of goods indicated in the needs assessment have to pay for it with extra work. Prices are low because a lot of used and repaired market economy goods are given out.

7.4.1 Under- and overconsumption

In the Planned Economy, everyone has his or her own chosen basket of goods from the needs assessment. If this is used up and consumption continues, this additional service must be paid for. In addition, production is increased due to overconsumption and the duty roster is automatically adjusted. The same applies in reverse for underconsumption. Overconsumption is when 10% more is consumed than planned. Underconsumption is reached at 10% less consumption. If this threshold is exceeded, there is an automatic report to the plenary assembly.

The needs assessment computer programme automatically detects when someone consumes more or less than they have indicated. Provided that overconsumption and underconsumption balance out for all consumers as a whole, the overconsumers and underconsumers receive news that their consumption patterns have been balanced out by other consumers. The computer programme keeps a digital consumption account for everyone, which the consumer can view via the Social Directory. Those who consume more or less than indicated and this consumption behaviour cannot be balanced by other consumers receive an automatic warning. The warning message is issued as soon as 5% over- or under-consumption has occurred for that person.

If 10% overconsumption occurs, the affected consumer must procure the goods or services himself in the market economy. At the cash registers, the overconsumption reached is automatically recognised and a sales stop applies to the affected person. No further goods or services of the Planned Economy will be issued. One possibility for affected consumers is also to work more in the corresponding work area to compensate for the extra work of others. The amount of work to be done is determined by the price in working hours. If affected consumers decide to buy, the price in national currency applies. Now it is up to the Social Villagers' will to work whether they want to do the extra work to earn the money or whether the consumer buys the product from the market economy.

If 10% underconsumption occurs, the affected consumer must sell the goods or services himself in the market economy or dispose of them at a cost. In order not to waste labour unnecessarily, the underconsumption must be reported in time so that production can be curtailed. If it is possible to sell the overproduction profitably in the market economy, production is not curbed, but a report is made to the plenary assembly. It decides whether the revenues are needed or whether more free time is brought forward.

The plenary assembly has the right to have over- and under-consumers indicated by the computer programme. These Social Villagers must then justify themselves and, if necessary, adjust their consumption demand or labour supply.

7.4.2 Consumption by guests and visitors

All services to visitors and residents are charged via their visitor card or social card on card readers so that the algorithm can record the time, type and quantity of a service in order to change the offer if necessary and adjust the duty rosters accordingly. Visitors are considered tourists. Demand can therefore fluctuate seasonally, which must be taken into account to avoid shortages. The algorithm plans visitor numbers based on the data collected from the identity cards and visitor or social cards. The decisive factors are where and when visitors come from, which residents have regular guests, how long these persons stay on average and how much they consume. The distance travelled from the place of residence to the Social Village is considered a gauge for the spontaneity index. Longer trips are less likely to be spontaneous.

The solvency index calculates the probability of whether a visitor will buy goods and services on site or bring his or her own consumer goods. To do this, the algorithm accesses the data that this visitor has already produced during past visits to the Social Village. For example, he could enter the dining room but not order anything there, but eat the food he brought with him, which is allowed. The algorithm evaluates this as an indication that the visitor is using consumer goods he brought himself. Accordingly, a lower demand is predicted.

7.5 Prices

The companies set prices for their goods and services and use the currency of the Planned Economy. The conversion rate into the national currency of the Social Market Economy is set by the Note-issuing Bank of the Planned Economy.[53] In the Planned Economy, the maxim of full employment applies, price stability is secondary, since prices in the Planned Economy correspond to the working hours required to

------

53 Ministry of Finance - 10.4 Note-issuing Banks

produce a service. This means that everyone should participate in the supply work, even if it takes longer overall to complete all the supply work.

Planned Businesses, state enterprises and Planned Enterprises form their prices together with the economic auditors of the Company Auditing Agency using scientifically developed formulas and factors. This is to ensure that the prices in each Social Village are as equal and comparable as possible. If possible, constant returns to scale should be achieved in every Social Village or company with the same work output. This means that with the same input of material and labour, the same service can be provided at the same price. Deviations due to different levels of education, professional experience, disability or age are accepted and, if necessary, additional workers are employed or moves are required.

Experimental Enterprises and Innovation Enterprises can set their own prices and receive support from the economic auditors of the Company Auditing Agency.

People's Innovation Company form monopoly prices but sell to Social Villagers at cost-covering price plus 10% profits.

Social Villagers can pay prices priced in working hours with their working hours in their work benefit account.

7.5.1 Pricing

The price is determined by the demanders determining their quantity and compiling their baskets of goods. They do this once a year in the needs assessment. Based on the given quantities, the suppliers determine what they have to do and how long they and the providers need to do it. The quantities of the demanders are now compared to the working hours of workers with different qualifications. Since the demanders are also the workers, they can determine their working hours through their demand.

Once the demanders have decided on a quantity, the companies calculate the costs of material and labour for the fixed quantity. They divide the costs by the quantity produced and add 10% to this amount as a reserve, which is the unit price.

7.5.1.1 Price-sales function

Based on the price, a demand function and a supply function are created. Demanders are asked in the needs assessment at what prices they would consume more or less of their basket of goods. This calculates the price elasticity of demand. Suppliers are asked in the needs assessment what quantity they could produce if the price were higher or lower. This calculates the price elasticity of supply. In order to be able to calculate a curve, 6 comparison prices are to be applied. A price that is 10%, 30%, 50% above and below the current price respectively. To improve measurement, the Company Auditing Agency manages its data from the audits of the companies and evaluates all data from the social card.

The price in the Planned Economy is the national currency of the Social Market Economy and the currency working hours. Prices in the Planned Economy are expressed in working hours and in the national currency of the Social Market Economy. For the calculation of the hourly prices, the working hours necessary for the provision are added up and the human capital factor is multiplied by the working hours. The economic auditors of the Company Auditing Agency are responsible for establishing the factors for the human capital factor.[54]

7.5.1.2 Pricing through working hours

The conversion of working hours into monetary value is done using the minimum wage per hour in the Social Market Economy. This minimum wage is multiplied by the human capital factor, which includes the training, responsibility and difficulty factors. This happens automatically for all Social Villagers and is adjusted for the individual's current health, age and qualifications and recorded on the Social Card. All time clocks record these factors and multiply the working time by them.

The factors become multipliers in the pricing. Thus, 3.5

54Ministry of Labour - 20.7.3.6.2.2 Measurement of currency Working hours working hours in a heart operation can become 52.5 hours worth of work for the physician performing the operation.[55] All goods and services that come from the Planned Economy are expressed in the national currency of the Social Market Economy and in working hours. This makes it possible for Social Villagers to trade these hourly amounts as digital currency on their Social Card. In the market economy, material resources are the scarce commodity that people compete to sell. In the Planned Economy, it is the working time in hours for which free time is sacrificed that is competed for in the scarce good of lifetime.

As a consequence, goods produced by employees with different levels of education would cost different amounts. The companies as price-forming suppliers remunerate each employee according to his or her human capital factor. However, the prices are formed from the average of all wages for employees plus 10% as excess capacity in order to be able to cushion fluctuations.

7.5.2 Balance of supply and demand

Balance is achieved when the Social Villagers agree with their shopping basket and duty roster. Since this agreement is negotiated only once a year as planned, there must be automation for the current year. The algorithm that was already used in the needs assessment works around the clock in a computer programme that measures demand and automatically adjusts supply accordingly. The measurement is done with the help of the social card via actual consumption at cash registers and doors, as well as by recording work performance at time clocks. If demand falls, the working hours in the duty roster are reduced in order to produce less. The same is true in reverse for an increase in demand. Price is used to manage demand towards surplus supplies and away

---

55 National currency (NW): 10NW * 2.5 (medical studies) * 3 (life or death) * 2 (3.5 hours of concentration, fine motor skills without trembling, work instructions to OR staff) = 150NW hourly pay
Working hours: 3.5 working hours (duration of surgery) * 2.5 (medical studies) * 3 (life or death) * 2 (3.5 hours of concentration, fine motor skills without trembling, work instructions to surgical staff) = 52.5 hours

from deficient supplies.

The programme automatically calculates which input factors are necessary to achieve the desired turnover and proposes the appropriate price. In the current year, the companies pay for their individual input factors. All these payments are recorded by the programme. All workers continuously enter their performance via the time clocks and the Company Auditing Agency protocol to receive their income. Social Villagers continuously acknowledge their consumption at the cash registers to receive their benefits. As long as everyone enters their data honestly, the computer programme can allocate labour and benefits in the best possible way according to given qualifications and interests. In order to take away the authority of having to trust the computer programme blindly, the source code must be made public. All criteria according to which the algorithm searches for and rates data must be published by the Ministry of Digital Affairs so that the Social Villagers can control them and, if necessary, change them through a veto quorum.

7.5.3 Input factors

Input factors are things that are necessary to produce goods or services. These are working hours, education, machines, buildings and raw materials such as electricity, water, air, earth or biomass. All input factors are dependent on the technological era in which they exist. The innovation auditors assign a future factor in their audit, which indicates whether the technology and production methods are backward or more productive. In order to be able to set prices and quantities, the input factors on the supply side are the limiting factors because they are finite.

The Company Auditing Agency measures all stocks and calculates factors for all things that have an influence on working time. With all input factors and their costs in working hours, the production function can be calculated. It indicates how long it takes to produce a certain quantity. Social Villagers can change the quantity in the needs assessment to see how much they have to work and weigh their needs for consumption and leisure.

7.5.3.1 Working time

In order to record the working time, each worker indicates how long he works via the time clock. The quantity produced during this time is read off a cash register. This makes it clear how long it took the worker to produce the quantity.
Persons who work particularly fast are visited and questioned by the Company Auditing Agency's economic auditors. If the auditors find a potentially innovative way of working, the workers are given a 360° helmet camera to document their work processes. If the economic auditors' evaluation reveals an innovative way of working, it is added to the Innovation Database and automatically shared via the Social Directory with all workers in other Social Villages who occupy the same job.

7.5.3.2 Training

The Ministry of Education states how long an educational qualification takes on average. The Company Auditing Agency calculates the education factor from this, which is multiplied by the working time to represent the time share for the duration of the training. In addition to education, the human capital factor also includes the factors of responsibility and difficulty that arise in a job. Together they make up the human capital factor.

7.5.3.3 Machines

Machines have a cost of acquisition and ongoing maintenance and operating costs. The purchase price is given in hours, which adds up the working hours to produce the machine, to produce building materials and to extract raw materials, and multiplies by the human capital factors of the workers involved. Maintenance costs are given in hours that maintenance takes and multiplied by the human capital factor. If material is used for operation, the costs are calculated as for the purchase price.

7.5.3.4 Building

When buildings, such as factories or shops, are constructed, working hours, including the human capital factor and material costs, are added to the purchase price in hours. Land in the Social Villages is owned by all residents of all Social Villages and has no price.

7.5.3.5 Raw materials

Raw materials include the costs of labour, materials and machinery to extract them. Since the Planned Economy forms a circular economy, only renewable raw materials or reusable raw materials are allowed for production purposes. Nature contributes with its ecosystem to the value creation. Excluded from this are recycled goods from the market economy, they are also considered permissible raw materials. These raw materials are cheaper because only the labour for collection and processing is estimated for them. Therefore, these raw materials are preferred.

7.5.3.6 Imports

Goods and services that the Planned Economy does not produce for cost reasons or cannot produce at all due to a lack of raw materials or skilled workers are given in market prices. Here it is observed what the Planned Economy could produce itself as a substitute and what skilled workers would have to be trained. As soon as the effort is worthwhile, the computer programme shows it and the imports are replaced by planning companies.

7.5.4 Measurement of the input factors

In order to be able to calculate quantities and prices, all input factors are measured regularly. Company Auditing Agency economic auditors measure individual input factors themselves on a random basis and otherwise rely on the workers' logs. The protocols are issued by the Company Auditing Agency to the workers and must be prepared within a specified period of time and handed in to the Company Auditing Agency by a specified date. These logs indicate which input factors were used during the period and what was produced with them. This is done for all Social Villagers who produce the same thing in order to have comparative values. Social Villagers cannot see each other's data to avoid manipulation and collusion. In order to keep this bureaucracy low, protocols only have to be made area-wide at the beginning until there is enough data to be able to simulate all workplaces. After that, spot checks can be made. Regular logs can be ordered in exceptional cases. Such exceptional cases can occur due to consumer complaints, doubts on the part of economic auditors or evidence of an increase in productivity due to an innovation. To digitise the measurement, glasses with built-in cameras to recognise completed activities or devices to capture bar codes can be issued. The measurements of input factors are flanked by the recording of hours on time clocks and the settled sales prices and unit numbers at the cash registers.

7.6 Duty roster[56]

The duty roster is the instrument to be able to support the supply in the Planned Economy through a division of labour by working Social Villagers. Together with the needs assessment, this results in the working plan. The rule here is that supply adjusts to demand and not vice versa. The Social Villagers determine their demand at plenary assemblies, knowing that they have to earn it through their own working hours. The Ministry of Planned Economy provides jobs through the state enterprises, Planned Businesses and Planned Enterprises,

---

56§230.2b Social Security

which provide the products of basic supply and the products of luxury supply desired by all.

How these positions are filled is decided democratically by the Social Villagers in the work choice through a digital interactive duty roster. The digital platform provides the Social Directory, where popular and unpopular services, times and colleagues are distributed fairly. The duty roster is automatically adjusted to fluctuations in demand. Digital currency immediately identifies deviations from needs assessment and adjusts duty periods. Automatically corrected duty rosters must be voted on at the next plenary assembly.

7.6.1 Digital duty roster

The digital duty roster of all Social Villages allows the residents to distribute their compulsory hours fairly and self-determined. It is a computer programme that can be accessed via the Social Directory. Users must log in with their profiles from the Persons Directory and Labour Directory. Based on the data, suitable services are proposed. In the event of a shortage of skilled workers, skilled workers are obliged to take on mainly those services for which they are most qualified.

All companies in Planned Economy have a profile in the Social Directory where they publish their duty rosters and individual jobs, including job descriptions and shifts.

An algorithm in the computer programme then searches all directories for data that can provide information about which services are suitable for a Social Villager. This computer programme also evaluates all working time accounts in order to have as few overtime or minus hours as possible, to be able to compensate for these and to make sufficient holidays possible.

The computer programme for the digital working plan is connected to all time clocks and cash registers in all Social Villages, so that fluctuations in demand can be detected automatically and supply adjusted accordingly. This makes it possible to avoid waste and shortages, which increases the work output per unit of time and thus increases free time.

7.6.2 Working hours account[57]

Social Villagers receive a working hours account for all companies they work for. Working hours are booked on the social card and can be viewed in the digital duty roster via the Social Directory. The booking is made when the social card is held in front of the time clock reader at the beginning and end of the service. Services can be performed at different speeds. The time clock readers of all Social Villages record the working hours performed and the payment readers record the amount of services performed during this time. This allows an average value to be calculated, which serves as a guideline as to how much time is needed for which service.

The working hours account automatically converts all work performance into a standardised work performance per hour. Social Villagers can also work faster or slower. It doesn't make any difference, what counts is the work done. All Social Villagers are credited with the same working hours for the same work performed.

The credit on the working hours account is posted to the work benefit account as wages at the end of the month. Social Villagers have to make sure that they enrol in enough services to get the working hours that correspond to their consumption. Which services they enrol in is up to them. As there will be more popular and less popular jobs, So-called work elections will be held.

7.6.2.1 Overtime

Those who work overtime either voluntarily take longer at work or have more to do. If someone has more to do, this is recognised by the computer programme, because firstly, more work is done at the same time, which is recognised by the cash registers and time clocks. Secondly, there are comparable jobs in other Social Villages, which are automatically compared. If there is so much to be done that a new job can be created, a note is automatically sent to the next plenary assembly. Involuntary overtime may be accumulated over one year.

57§219.3b Central Bank and Currency Policy

Overtime can be reduced in consultation with the enterprise or the company. The possible dates for the reduction of overtime are automatically displayed to the affected person by the computer programme of the digital duty roster. 12 hours of overtime may be taken into the next year. If a sanction involving overtime has been imposed, overtime may be redeemed for it.

7.6.2.2 New job

As soon as overtime regularly accrues and in its total from all affected employees from the working hours makes up a part-time position, a new worker must be scheduled for this job. The job is automatically brought in during the next needs assessment and displayed as new. It will be included in the next year's duty roster if the Social Villagers are in favour. If this is rejected and in the following year overtime is again reached to the extent of a part-time job or even more, a new job must be scheduled, the price increased or consumption restricted.

7.6.2.3 Holiday

Anyone wishing to take leave must fill out an application in the Social Directory and indicate the date in it. 80% of the leave days must already be indicated by the deadline of the needs analysis. The digital duty roster is automatically checked and, if necessary, a representation is appointed. Every Social Villager is entitled to 10 days' leave per year in the basic supply work area. In the work area luxury supply it is 20 days.

7.6.3 Jobs / labour supply

Companies provide the supply of jobs to be filled by Social Villagers to meet the needs assessment. They do whatever is necessary to fulfil the working plan. Social Villagers create the working plan through the needs assessment and their entries in the digital duty roster. For employers, the results of the needs assessment are crucial. They calculate how many workers they need to provide a supply that meets demand based on the goods and services demanded. Whether these calculations are correct, i.e. there are no losses, shortages or surpluses over 10%, is checked by the Company Auditing Agency's economic auditors.[58]

Each service receives a profile in the virtual duty roster of the Social Directory. On the profile, the activities and duty periods to be performed are described and shown as a video. It also indicates the maximum number of persons who can share this workplace and whether professional qualifications are necessary. For example, it is possible to use every other worker every hour when washing dishes in the canteen kitchen. In infant care, for example, this would not be possible, neither such a frequently changing caregiver, nor professionally untrained staff.

What must be done as a minimum in a working hour is proposed by the employer, rated by the employee and finalised by the economic auditors of the Company Auditing Agency[59] . The Ministry of Planned Economy and the plenary assembly of the affected Social Village have a right of veto. Thus, the working content of a working hour can be precisely determined in the course of a solution finding at the plenary assembly.

Companies can also enter seasonal overtime or undertime for different months and thus request more or fewer working hours. In general, companies are allowed to flexibly adapt to demand. The personal and digital needs assessment is intended to avoid large fluctuations with shortages or overproduction. The fluctuating number of working hours means more or less free time for all residents while supporting the same level of supply.

7.6.3.1 Labour shortage

If there is a shortage of labour in the work area of basic supply, the number of hours per week is increased for the remaining people who are able to work. This may be the case if there

---

58 Ministry of Labour - 20.7.3.6.1.2 Audit of the duty roster
59 Ministry of Labour - 20.7.3.6.1.4 Audit of working hours

are many children, disabled and sick people living in a Social Village. The Social Villages ensure a balance among themselves so that the workload is similar in all Social Villages. This may require Social Villagers to move. The Ministry of Planned Economy submits the motions and the plenary assembly of the affected Social Village votes on it. If many Social Villagers move out, capacity is readjusted and businesses or houses are closed down or revived.

7.6.4 Labour choice / labour demand

In labour choice, the demand for labour meets the supply of labour. Demanders are the Social Villagers who are faced with the election of which services they would like to fill. Usually, Social Villagers take on several services to diversify their daily work. Not everyone enjoys every activity equally. Social Villagers should decide for themselves which jobs they enjoy the most and work there. However, there will always be activities that no one likes. The choice of work takes these preferences of the residents into account. The work elections take place every year for needs assessment. There are three rounds of elections.

In the first round, everyone indicates their first, second and third preference, which work they like best and which work they like least. Likewise, information can be given about who is more of a morning person or a night person, and with which colleagues one would like to work and with whom one would not.

An algorithm stores the data and distributes the services. The ideal case is that everyone only does popular services, because all residents have different preferences. Otherwise, care is taken that, if possible, no one only does unpopular services, but that popular and unpopular services alternate for one worker. Those who do more unpopular than popular services receive one bonus point per unpopular service for the next choice of work.

In the second round, bonus points from previous years can be redeemed. There is a new count with blocked works. Social Villagers can spend their bonus points to get certain jobs or not get certain jobs. All participants who want to fill the same job or not duel each other with bonus points. Each bonus point beats another. Whoever is the first to run out of bonus points must take an unpopular job. Whoever is the last to have bonus points left gets to take the popular job. Those who chose these jobs in the first round must now take on the jobs that were rejected with bonus points. The work period ends with the next work election next year.

In the third round, the duty periods are assigned. Everyone enters all possible time periods into an input mask. From past voting, the algorithm has stored who is more of a morning person or a night person and distributes the duty periods accordingly.

A free exchange phase now follows within one day. In this phase, all work and all duty periods can be exchanged, provided both exchange partners agree and have the necessary qualifications.

7.6.4.1 Wishes

Through the digital duty roster, requests for leave days, colleagues, duty periods and duty stations can be entered, with first, second and third requests. An algorithm makes proposals to each Social Villager on how the affected person should do the least unpopular work and get to their monthly hours as quickly as possible or as slowly as possible. There is also a function where the algorithm can link the duty roster from companies in the Planned Economy, the market economy or timetables from educational institutions attended. In this way, several jobs and educational qualifications can be managed at the same time.

7.6.4.2 Professionals

Specialists must complete their compulsory hours in their specialist department, unless there is an oversupply of specialists in that specialist department. If there is an oversupply, the skilled workers vote among themselves on who would like to do the work and who would rather do their working hours in another activity. If there is a shortage of skilled workers, Social Villagers must seek further training. If not enough Social Villagers declare their willingness to do so, the decision is made by lot. In the Social Directory, there is a digital lottery procedure that all residents can carry out if they cannot come to an amicable agreement without causing disappointment in the personal relationship. Those who do not wish to accept their lot can use their bonus points for this purpose and duel with all those who have also drawn the lot to further their education. The lottery will be repeated when a sufficient number of participants have no more bonus points.

7.6.4.3 Team

In the duty roster, friends or couples can enter joint services and duty periods with the addition of wanting to work in the team. All persons who want to work in the team must give their consent via the Social Directory. Those who want to work together can indicate this in the query and the algorithm searches for two free jobs on the same shift or in the same company.

7.6.4.4 Tandem

Several persons can join together to form tandem teams. They flexibly take over each other's shifts. This can be two part-time positions or one full-time position. The algorithm automatically searches for jobs with the necessary qualifications of all participating persons. All participants in the tandem teams must give their consent via the Social Directory.

7.6.4.5 Exchange

Duty periods can be swapped at any time, provided this is agreed with the team. Swapping of services is only possible after consultation with the management, provided that all swapping partners agree.

8 Ownership

The personal property of the Social Villagers is their income, their assets in the People's Bank account, their belongings in their flat, room or warehouse, all the data generated by them, and their learning and labour. Their common property is the Social Villages, which they have administered by directly elected politicians. Excluded from this ownership are all state enterprises of the other ministries, namely education, health, security, justice, family, finance and state organisation, which are people's property.

8.1 Private sources of income

Social Villagers are paid for their compulsory hours in the work area of basic supply with baskets of goods to meet basic needs. As wages in the work area luxury supply, they receive working hours with which they can purchase goods of luxury supply. For exports to the market economy, they receive a share of the profits, which is in proportion to the working hours worked personally and the working hours worked by all employees.

The community of Social Villagers owns all the things that are available in the Social Village and is allowed to make profits with them as long as at least the needs according to the needs assessment are met. Markets and auctions are held where all companies of the work area luxury supply and Social Villagers are allowed to offer their goods and services. These events take place on the open day. The items are auctioned English[60] or Dutch[61] . This is up to the sellers to decide. Otherwise, the marketing can be done via the Labour Directory or in the Social Market.

---

60 (Highest bidder / outbid from starting price until time runs out)
61 (From the start time, the price decreases continuously until the end, the first to strike wins).

8.2 Income

The Social Villagers' income is generated by their work performance in the two work areas. The income from compulsory work in the basic supply work area corresponds to the services provided by the state enterprises, Planned Businesses and Planned Enterprises. Payment is made in kind, such as food and drink, ordered baskets of goods, such as hygiene articles or clothing, and services, such as washing clothes or cutting hair. If the duty roster for compulsory work was not fulfilled in the previous month, benefits are reduced in the following month and, if necessary, a penalty is imposed. The income from gainful employment in the luxury supply work area corresponds to the profit sharing in Planned Enterprises, Experimental Enterprises and Innovation Enterprises as well as the monthly wage including annual bonus in a People's Innovation Company. Remuneration is paid through a transfer to the People's Bank account or the work benefit account. The work benefit account is held in the digital currency of the Planned Economy. This income comes from working in Planned Enterprise, Experimental Enterprise or Innovation Enterprise to provide the Social Villagers with luxury goods that they have requested in the needs assessment. The People's Bank account can be held with all currencies of the world on individual sub-accounts. This income arises from the sale of innovations, goods and services to the market economy or abroad. The sales proceeds are paid out to the workers as foreign currency after deduction of taxes and costs. If surpluses from the basic supply work area are sold, the Social Village receives these revenues. If surpluses from the work area of luxury supply are sold, all those who have worked on it receive the share that corresponds to their work performance and is democratically negotiated with their colleagues.

8.2.1 Unconditional Basic Income

The Unconditional Basic Income[62] is credited to the domestic Social Villagers monthly on their Social Card. At least 50% of the amount must be deposited in the People's Bank account under the heading of old-age provision. The Social Villagers can freely dispose of the remaining amount.

As their own basic income, Planned Businesses and Planned Enterprises distribute their revenues from machine labour, which remain after deducting machine fees[63] . In basic supply, the revenues are paid out as compulsory working hours. Social Villagers thus get more free time because basic supply work has been automated. In luxury supply, the amount is paid out in working hours when the products from machine work in Planned Economy have been consumed for luxury supply. Social Villagers are thus given the opportunity to buy Planned Economy products for luxury supply. The amount is paid in the currency of the market economy when the products have been sold there. Therefore, the Planned Economy's Unconditional Basic Income consists of working hours and foreign exchange.

8.2.2 Child benefit

The child benefit is the same as for all other children inland.[64] It is used entirely to cover the costs of a child's stay in the Social Village. It does not play a role whether the child lives with the parents or in the children's home. For the general calculation of the amount of the child benefit, the care situation of a child in the children's home is assumed. The Ministry of Health is responsible for assessing the amount of need for children per year of life up to the age of majority. This information is used to determine the need for housing, food, clothing, hygiene, health care and education. Children are allowed to participate in the needs assessment to indicate their demand for recreation.

---

62 Ministry of Finance - 6 Unconditional Basic Income
63 Ministry of Finance - 6.1 Machine Fees
64 Ministry of Family Affairs - 8.4 Child benefit

8.3 Work benefit account[65]

Social Villagers receive a work benefit account with three sub-accounts at the People's Bank. The first two are kept in the digital currency of Planned Economy, the third in the currencies of Social Market Economy and Free Market Economy. The first sub-account is for compulsory work in the basic supply work area. The second is for voluntary work in the luxury supply work area. The third is for revenues from trade with the market economy.

Fulfilment of compulsory work according to the duty roster counts as credit for the purpose of receiving basic supply benefits. These amounts can only be spent in the following month.

Those who work for luxury supply companies receive working hours and can use them to buy luxury supply products made in companies of the luxury supply work area.

Those who work for luxury supply companies that export to the market economy are paid a share of the profits in the currency that was used to pay for the product. With this money, all kinds of things can be bought.

If Experimental Enterprises, Innovation Enterprises or People's Innovation Companies also produce for needs assessment, the equivalent value of the products must be paid in working hours. Conversely, this means that only as many products can be sold in working hours as Social Villagers have worked with. For example, if one wants to buy a flying car from the People's Innovation Company flying car and pay for it in working hours, the People's Innovation Company flying car must employ as many Social Villagers as there are working hours in the production. Assuming a flying car costs 100,000 working hours and the People's Innovation Company flying car employs 1000 Social Villagers working 40 hours per week, then a flying car could be paid for in working hours every 2.5 weeks. The prerequisite for this is that the employees have their wages paid in working hours by the People's Innovation Company. The wage is then calculated by multiplying the number of hours worked per week by the human capital factor calculated by the Company Auditing Agency's economic

65§219.3b Central Bank and Currency Policy

auditors.

9 Work area basic supply[66]

The work area of basic supply is the heart of the Planned Economy, because without this work area the Social Villagers cannot survive and the rest of the Planned Economy cannot exist. Therefore, the working hours needed to provide basic supply are considered compulsory working hours. All Social Villagers are obliged to work them, but they decide together democratically how much and what is to be done where and when. To do this, they use the needs assessment and the digital duty roster. In the needs assessment, the quantities and working hours for the basic necessities are determined.

The work area of basic supply includes state enterprises, Planned Businesses and partly also Planned Enterprises. They provide goods and services to ensure basic necessity. All operations beyond this are subject to guaranteeing the basic supply of all Social Villages. No one is allowed to freeze or starve to death in the Social Villages.

9.1 Basic supply policy

The first priority is to produce the basic supply and do the weekly compulsory work according to the duty roster. After that, either leisure time or work in luxury supply is possible. The income consists of benefits that each Social Villager has wished for in the needs assessment and voted for at the plenary assembly. The services are provided by the companies in the basic supply work area. Necessary goods and services for basic supply are produced by Planned Enterprises and provided by Planned Businesses. Planned Enterprises may also produce for the market economy as long as this does not jeopardise basic supply.

66§210,2,5 Principles of economic order: BV Art. 94, §230,2c Social security: BV Art. 112

9.2 Basic necessity

Basic necessities are provided by the Minister of Planned Economy, his deputies and the politicians for housing, food, clothing and hygiene. Social Villagers are responsible for completing compulsory working hours in Social Service, Hotel, Moving, Housing, Market Garden, Commercial Kitchen, Supply Centre, Central Store, Garment Factory, Upgrading Company, Laundry and Planned Enterprise for specialisation of individual Social Villages.

Every Social Villager is entitled to the same level of clothing, furniture and household items. The number of basic necessities is determined by the Social Villagers in the needs assessment. For example, 6 pairs of trousers are in the basic necessity. If a pair of trousers is broken or unpopular, they can be exchanged for another pair of used trousers or new trousers at the social market. The same applies to all other items in the basic necessity.

Consumables, such as toothpaste, are only released for purchase in limited numbers in time quotas on the social card. For example, once a month a tube of toothpaste can be picked up at the social market with the Social Card. The consumer goods of the basic necessities are included in the income from the basic supply work area and do not have to be paid for.

In addition, the basic necessities are supplemented by the state enterprises of the ministries of labour, education, family, finance, health, infrastructure, innovation, integration, intranet, justice, media, security and state organisation. Social Villagers perform compulsory working hours for the Ministries in the Employment Exchange, Educational Institutions, Children's House, Leisure Centre, People's Bank Branch, Health Centre, House for Disabled People, Energy Centre, Caretaker's Office, Workshop, Modernisation Company, Research Community, Asylum Sponsorship, Intranet Café, Court of Aldermen, Radio and TV Channel, Security Centre and Town Hall. There is no cap on the use of state services, but it can be introduced in a plenary assembly and limited in time.

9.3 Staff

The basic supply staff consists of all Social Villagers from birth to death. Until the age of majority, work performance consists of education and, with increasing abilities, increasingly more working hours per week. The working hours per week correspond to the age in years, but only start at the age of 6. For example, a 15-year-old would have to work 15 hours per week in the work area of basic supply.

Suitable activities are reserved in the duty roster for pregnant women, senior citizens, disabled people and people with illnesses. The staff consists of beginners, experienced and skilled workers. Beginners are all unskilled Social Villagers. Experienced staff are those who have already successfully carried out an activity 3 times. Skilled workers are all Social Villagers who have work experience in the field or have completed relevant training. Journeymen and master's craftspersons train other workers. If there are no skilled workers in the field, skilled workers are purchased until enough Social Villagers have been trained at the Education Centre.

9.3.1 Recruitment in the basic supply

Basic supply companies report vacancies to the Social Village Town Hall at the Ministry of Labour office or through the Labour Directory. The Company Auditing Agency[67] checks whether another job is needed or whether there are enough skilled workers. Trained professionals are always employed in the areas in which they have been trained. If there are enough skilled workers in one post, the skilled workers may also choose another job in the basic supply work area. If favouritism is found, the employment relationship must be changed according to the Company Auditing Agency's requirements. If favouritism is repeatedly found, charges of favouritism will be brought.[68]

---

67 Ministry of Labour - 20.7.3.6.1.1 Audit of the need for workers in basic supply
68 Ministry of Justice - 8.16.4 Favouritism

9.3.2 Authority

In the enterprises, the authority to give instructions applies to all skilled trained workers vis-à-vis workers without professional training. Every worker has the right to complete the necessary vocational training in the Social Village to become authorised to give instructions. In the case of equal professional qualifications, the equal working method in a team and the independent working method in the case of self-employed workers applies.

9.3.3 Distribution of working hours

The number of working hours depends on the work required for basic supply. The amount of working hours for each individual is based on the number of Social Villagers available. All working hours per week of all services are divided by the total number of Social Villagers available to work. This gives the number of hours per week per person. Depending on age or impairments, only certain activities can be performed. A medical certificate from the health centre is required for this. Depending on qualifications, skilled work can also be carried out. A final testimonial from a recognised educational institution is required for this.

9.3.4 Compulsory working hours

All Social Villagers must cover a minimum number of work activities in the work area of basic supply in order to ensure the Self-sufficiency of a Social Village.
All Social Villagers are obliged to do a certain amount of work per week in the work area of basic supply. The amount of work per Social Villager depends on how many workers are available in the Social Village to do the necessary work. The Social Villagers determine the nature and extent of the work in the annual needs assessment or as needed at the plenary assembly. Producing residents and businesses deliver their earnings to the centres, where they are distributed to all Social Villagers. Other businesses support the Social Villagers with

services, such as the caretaker's office.

Those who have worked all compulsory working hours for basic supply in the past month will get admission to basic supply benefits in the next month. Those who have worked less will receive cuts and have to work the hours in the following month. Those who receive cuts are no longer entitled to visits to the hairdresser, the clothing ration for that year is halved and admission to the leisure park is blocked until the hours have been made up. If this occurs in another month, the person affected must testify before the plenary assembly and can be charged with theft.

9.3.5 Rating

How the basic supply was done can be indicated in the Social Directory via the profile of the person on duty. Customers or colleagues can thus rate whether the work performance was satisfactory. Anyone who repeatedly receives poor ratings must exchange with the person who receives good ratings for the same service. Those who repeatedly receive poor ratings must justify themselves before the next plenary assembly. The motions will be submitted automatically by the Social Directory as soon as the quorum of 60% of bad ratings has been reached. If the ratings were given to discredit someone, those who gave the ratings must testify before the plenary assembly. If it is found that the ratings were falsified, charges of blasphemy and bullying will be brought.[69] The plenary assembly can decide on punitive measures against the accused if a badly rated person repeatedly comes forward. The legal process is open to the accused.

9.3.6 Punitive measures

Anyone who does not perform his or her compulsory work for basic supply properly can be given a warning. Warning letters are reports from affected persons about poor work performance. Several warnings result in employment bans

---

69 Ministry of Justice - 8.16.5 Blasphemy

at that workplace and 2 more working hours per week for 4 months at a centre with opening hours.

Those who do not complete their work in full have to take on another job the following week. In return, other employees get time off. Who gets time off depends on the time account of the employees who have previously compensated or had to endure the absence.

Punishment work should be done where possible, where a lot of overtime can be reduced. The penalty worker then replaces the usual worker who can reduce overtime during this time.

Anyone who has built up so many minus hours in their time account that they have missed a week of work must be detained for a week in the security centre.

Anyone who has not completed one month's working hours in one year is liable to detention for one month in the following year.

Those who completely refuse to work in the work area of basic supply have to move out of the Social Village. Moving in again is only possible after 10 years.

9.3.7 Protection against dismissal

In the work area of basic supply, one cannot be dismissed, but only punitive transferred. Those who perform their work poorly are warned. Clients or employees authorised to give instructions can complain about the deficiencies on the profile in the Social Directory. As soon as a quorum of 60% dissatisfied affected persons is met, a vote on a punitive transfer is taken at the plenary assembly. Compulsory work that is regularly avoided by Social Villagers in the duty roster is selected as a job for punitive transfer. In the next year, the duty roster can be filled without any restrictions. However, those who have been punitive transferred 3 times are no longer allowed to select this activity in the duty roster.

9.3.8 Parental protection[70]

When parents have a child, parental protection comes into effect. For the mother, from the 4th month of pregnancy onwards, certain work, as determined by the Institute of Occupational Health[71] , is considered unacceptable. From the time of birth, a parental leave of 24 months applies, which must be shared by both parents. This is to ensure that in the first two most formative years of a human life, parents have sufficient time for their offspring and that one parent can always be with the child to create a sense of primal trust in the child. Compulsory work is reduced by 50% for both parents, a move to the family home is made before the birth and the personal available basket of goods is extended to include the standard benefits of parental leave. If the parents still work in the work area of luxury supply, this work must also be reduced by 50% by each parent, unless this would jeopardise a company newly established by at least one parent.

Parents receive as compulsory work from the 4th month of pregnancy attendance at courses in the children's home and training in the educational institution on the subject of pregnancy and parenting. During the parental leave, these education and experience measures are to be attended several times a week with the child. This is followed by annual training measures, which are attended with the children in order to be able to explain the developmental stages on an ongoing basis and give everyday advice.

Social Villagers who want to become parents can save this on their Social Card and receive proposals for diet and exercise that they can have automatically implemented. For example, certain food and drinks will then no longer be offered to you in the supply centre and drugs will no longer be dispensed in the pharmacy. For men, this period applies three months before conception because sperm production takes that long. For women, an adapted diet and exercise plan applies from the time pregnancy is established.

---

70 §234.4 Children's rights, child benefit and parental protection
71 Ministry of Health - 4.5.5 Institute of Occupational Health

9.3.9 Holidays

Two days a week are free of work, one of which is Sunday. The plenary assemblies take place on Sunday. Depending on the workload and demand, more days a week can be off. All residents are allowed to choose a day in the week on which they want to have time off and must schedule the services in their duty roster accordingly. If they have entered this information in the digital duty roster, the computer programme automatically takes this wish into account. Otherwise, all days set by the Ministry of Labour are considered public holidays.[72]

9.3.10 Holiday

All Social Villagers are entitled to 10 days holiday per year. Those who wish to take a holiday abroad must have sufficient foreign currency to book the trip in the market economy. All Social Villagers are entitled to 7 days holiday per year in a Social Village of their election. The Social Villages on the coasts, large lakes and in the mountains have businesses for tourism. Holidays are provided by the Social Service if there is sufficient demand, and state transport can be used free of charge for individual trips to holiday social villages. In voting with the Minister for Planned Economy, Social Villagers can extend holiday entitlements if the economic situation permits.

9.4 Planned Business

Planned Businesses are exclusively administered by the Ministry of Planned Economy and the Housing, Food, Clothing and Sanitation politicians and run by Social Villagers. Planned Businesses are either purpose-built or located in centres. In the buildings of the Planned Business basic supply work area, the house rules of the respective Planned Business or the residential buildings apply. These house rules are jointly voted on by the residents or users and staff. The Company Auditing Agency[73] has the right to insert binding passages into

---

72Ministry of Labour - 14.1 Public holidays
73Ministry of Labour - 20.7.2 Health auditor

the house rules that serve occupational safety.

9.4.1 Social Service

The Social Service is available to Social Villagers at the gate of each Social Village. Otherwise, its staff is deployed throughout the Social Village. The Social Service is mainly responsible for house management and logistics. It also organises short-, medium- and long-term stays in the Social Village. The Social Service organises the moves of residents and companies as well as logistics and transport of Social Villagers, Social Commuters, supplies, food and consumer goods. It enables Social Villagers and Social Commuters to rent and use the materials and premises in the Social Village. Those who use the services of the Social Service must acknowledge this with their Social Card.

The military's supply structures, which exist between the barracks, are used for the political management of operations between the Social Villages. Vehicles accessed by the Social Service are vehicles used in disaster and war situations. Therefore, some of the vehicles are painted in camouflage colours.

The Social Service is responsible for the administration of all buildings in the Social Village. The Social Service is responsible for the operation of the central warehouse and the motor pool. Moves or shuttles of persons or goods are organised and carried out by the Social Service. In the annual needs assessment, the positions in the duty roster and the acquisition and maintenance costs are included in the expenditure of the work areas for basic supply and luxury supply.

The "motor pool" is also, like "supply", a term from the politician's management of the military. The motor pool consists of cars, trucks and buses of various sizes with more or less seating capacity. The Social Service uses and maintains these vehicles in peacetime for the benefit of all Social Villagers. The Social Service, in cooperation with the Ministry of Infrastructure, ensures a smooth transfer of goods and services between the Social Villages. State local and long-distance transport connections are available to Social Villagers free of charge.

9.4.2 Community centre

The community hall is a mixture of a stadium and a parliament building. It has a stage and a grandstand. Ideally, it should offer space for all Social Villagers. The community hall is administered by the Social Service and can be booked by all Social Villagers. The clubs, for example for theatre or music, can present their art here. The ministries and Social Villagers can hold plenary assemblies and committees here to organise living together in a direct democratic way.

9.4.3 Commercial kitchen

The commercial kitchen has craftsperson equipment to turn plants and animals into food. The commercial kitchen building houses the butchery, bakery, dairy, fruit and vegetable collection point, kitchen and dishwashing department. These institutions are able to produce food from animals and plants, as well as put waste through a reprocessing cycle and clean devices. Biodegradable waste is collected and converted into electricity, heat and fertiliser in the biogas plant.

In the building or in an annex is the large dining hall, which is open around the clock and has seating for 25% of the Social Villagers. A buffet is offered around the clock, which changes according to the time of day and contains a standardised assortment of food that can be taken away and can be kept for at least one day without refrigeration. The food can also be taken away. A picnic basket is lent out for this purpose, equipped with the usual cutlery and special containers for the food. In case of loss or damage, the replacement value must be paid in working hours or paid.

When entering and leaving the dining hall and at the end of the meal service, the social card must be passed through a reader. It records who is in the dining hall, when, for how long and what is eaten. Borrowed picnic baskets are also recorded there. All data is continuously evaluated by the needs assessment algorithm in order to adjust the offer if necessary. The Social Villagers can request food in the Social Directory under the heading "Kitchen", rate tasted meals and make suggestions for improvement to the team of the commercial kitchen. This data collection is intended to avoid food not being available in sufficient quantities at peak times, or too much having to be thrown away. In general, as much food as necessary should be left on display until it has been picked up. Edible food should not be discarded. If a meal did not taste good, it will be prepared differently and offered the following day. Complaints are consciously accepted in order to avoid mass throwing away of food. Consumers should participate digitally to avoid having to work longer in the basic supply work area because food production has to be ramped up due to unused disposal.

Supermarkets and canteens from the market economy supply the Social Villages with their edible leftovers and can arrange collection times with the Social Service. Packaged goods that are suitable for direct consumption are made available to the social market. On the day of the expiry date, all this food from the social market must be processed in the commercial kitchen. Packaged food is not allowed in the biogas plant, it must be unpacked beforehand. If this is not possible, they have to go to the waste incinerator.

9.4.4 Supply centre

The supply centre provides goods and services for regular needs. Each Social Village plans its needs independently through direct democracy. The supply centre has at least a hairdresser's, a kiosk, a cinema, a bar, a discotheque and a social market.

9.4.4.1 Social Market

The supermarket in the Social Village is called the Social Market. There you can get consumer goods and donated, repaired or used goods. Donated goods and food come from the overproduction of the market economy. Repaired goods come from bulky waste collections in the market economy. Second-hand goods come from all Social Villages. Local second-hand goods are displayed in the local Social Market and are digitally offered in the Social Directory together with all second-hand goods from the Social Villages. Each social market has a camera robot that films the stocks in the shop and in the warehouse before and after closing time and thus updates the online shop of the social market.

The social market has an order catalogue with all goods of the Planned Economy. Ordered goods are dispatched during the regular logistics runs between the Social Villages.

New goods from the market economy are purchased through buyer associations and delivered to the social market or directly to the companies. If Social Villagers identify certain products in the needs assessment that are produced in Planned Enterprises, they are available in the Social Market but have to be pre-ordered.

9.4.4.2 Buyers' associations

Buyers' associations can be formed in the Social Market. This can be done firstly via a wish list posted in the market and secondly in the Social Directory. Residents enter the goods or services they would like to buy and can also raise the money for. This list can be accessed in the Social Directory via the profile page of the Social Market. Links can be added from the intranet or internet where the good or service with the best value for money has been found. All buyers vote on exactly which good or service to buy. They also select a responsible person who will send a request to the seller asking by what percentage the price will drop if the specified number of units is purchased. The seller's stated price must be covered by sufficient foreign exchange reserves of all members of the buyers' association. The chosen responsible buyer may process the purchase and must check the order on receipt and make a complaint if necessary. In relation to the seller from the market economy, the Ministry of Planned Economy acts as the buyer, and the responsible person is a deputy of the

Ministry of Planned Economy elected for this procedure. This data is automatically fed into the upcoming needs assessment to investigate whether a Planned Enterprise would cost less foreign exchange and to vote on whether it should be established.

9.4.4.2.1 Buyer

Buyers can be persons who need goods or services from the market economy for their private life or for their business life. Companies or businesses should only buy goods or services from the market economy if they are not available in the Planned Economy. Imports from the market economy can be financed either by tax revenues from the Ministry of Planned Economy or by exports from the luxury supply work area and surpluses from the basic supply work area. If tax money is to be used, this expenditure must be approved in the annual needs assessment.

9.4.4.2.2 Example

For example, USB memory sticks are ordered from all Social Villages. 22 000 Social Villagers from all over the country have agreed on the size of 64GB and can pay a maximum of 10 Dollars per piece for it. The chosen purchasing officer now sends out a request for proposal to the cheapest supplier(s) and obtains bids. The purchasing officer's starting bid is 5 Dollars per piece and the final negotiated price is 7.50 Dollars per piece, which the Social Villagers have to pay immediately by People's Bank transfer.

9.4.5 Caretaker's office

The caretaker's office has craftsperson equipment to renovate and build houses and roads. The caretaker's office building houses the reception, the changing room and the central store. Any necessary repairs or unfinished services can be reported at the reception. Work clothes are available in the locker room and the duty roster for the sweeping weeks of all buildings is posted. The central warehouse stocks furniture, institutions and fittings to equip entire households. The central warehouse is also used by the trades as a store for their building materials and materials for constructing buildings, roads and pipelines. The caretaker's office is also responsible for waste collection. In the central warehouse, the waste is collected and either converted into electricity by the Energy Centre or transported away to be processed in a Planned Enterprise.

9.4.5.1 Caretaker[74]

The caretakers of all houses have their camp in the caretaker's office. The caretaker provides help with necessary repairs and ensures that sweeping services are properly carried out. The Education Centre offers further training for caretakers to be able to carry out simple repairs safely and quickly.

The caretaker's office has booking rights for craftspersons of the Planned Economy. Repairs or structural measures that caretakers cannot carry out are carried out by craft businesses. At a caretakers' conference, there is an exchange about work equipment and work services and motions are made to the Ministry of Planned Economy for contributions in kind. The caretakers' conference is held at least once a quarter. Caretakers also look after residential and commercial buildings on a rotating basis. They are responsible for maintenance and may request additional working hours in the work area basic supply in the caretakers' conference, if this is necessary for an activity. The caretakers' conference is also responsible for the construction of new buildings. A new building must firstly be decided by the plenary assembly, secondly the need must be confirmed by the caretakers' conference and thirdly it must be drawn up by the architects of the Ministry of Infrastructure and approved at a plenary assembly. The caretakers' conference can use the manpower of all learners in the ninth and tenth learning years once a year on one day to repair or extend buildings. Alternatively, building can be done in the school subject "Building a House". If there is not enough space in a

74§226,1,3 Housing and home ownership promotion: BV Art. 108

Social Village, this can be reported to the state administration so that new land around the Social Village can be bought to expand it or a new Social Village can be built elsewhere.

9.4.5.2 Refuse collection

The first to sixth learning years take turns in sweeping and collecting rubbish during yard breaks and on excursions. This is to collect carelessly discarded rubbish and to create understanding among the children for the prohibition of careless disposal.

9.4.5.3 Sweep week

The sweeping week means the weekly cleaning of the houses and roads. This includes tidying, cleaning, sweeping and dusting in all rooms, sweeping streets and clearing snow, emptying all rubbish bins and sorting rubbish in the rubbish dump at the central depot. The sweeping duty has to be done by all Social Villagers and changes workers weekly.

9.4.6 Laundry

The laundry has craftsperson equipment to clean textiles, objects and buildings. The laundry building houses rooms with washing machines, dryers and ironing stations. All textiles from all buildings are washed and dried there. The building residents decide independently whether everyone washes and dries their own laundry in the laundry rooms or whether the responsibility should rotate within the building. Excluded from the washing of private laundry are any other textiles from the centres, businesses and companies. The washing of this laundry is done via the central duty roster of the work area basic supply.

The laundry also uses the central store for washing, cleaning and dishwashing detergents, cleaning trolleys, street sweepers and street clearers during snowfall. Next to the warehouse is the changing room for sweepers on duty, who can lend out work clothes and cleaning items.

9.4.7 Central warehouse

The central warehouse consists of a high-bay warehouse and a reception area where every Social Villager can lend out anything with their social card. Consumables are issued according to scheduled annual needs assessment. The reception is manned around the clock by a social service worker who administers the issue and return and checks damage and stocks. The machines in the central warehouse are usually multi-purpose to serve several farms. This makes it easier to adapt the number of machines to increasing demand in order to increase availability.

9.4.8 Workshop

The workshop of the Social Village is a factory hall near the central warehouse, which can be equipped with different tools and machines from the central warehouse. As basic necessities, each workshop has a 3D printer, a press, an oven and a CNC milling machine. It should be possible to build and repair any machine and all standard parts from the central warehouse in the workshop.

The workshop is a Planned Enterprise of the Ministry of Innovation and is administered by the Social Service. The first priority right of use is for repairing the machine stocks of the central warehouse, followed by a list in which companies from the two work areas and Social Villagers can register. If the waiting list for a workshop place is so long that one has to wait longer than 6 weeks, the issue will be negotiated at the next plenary assembly. If necessary, another workshop can be built if all residents in the luxury supply work area earn money to buy equipment and if all residents in the basic supply work area work more to compensate for the loss of the workers building the new workshop.

Social Villagers can learn skills for specific repairs at the Education Centre or in the Knowledge Directory and try them out in the workshop. Anyone who has skills in handling the workshop and certain machines or materials should indicate this in the Social Directory. Users of the workshop can ask this person if they can help them and what they expect in return. The workshop is used for the rare construction and repair of parts and devices of the companies of both work areas, for the upgrading of bulky waste as well as for the repair of goods of the Social Villagers. It is expressly desired that Social Villagers can exchange ideas and plans, form groups and realise their projects. However, this is not compulsory.

10 Work area luxury supply[75]

The luxury supply work area is open to all Social Villagers after the basic supply work area has been served. The luxury supply work area is for Social Villagers to earn working hours or money to buy or save consumer goods. The luxury supply work area includes companies set up either by the Ministry of Planned Economy, Social Villagers or the Ministry of Innovation. These are Planned Enterprise, Experimental Enterprise, Innovation Enterprise and People's Innovation Company.

People's Innovation Companies do not necessarily have to be based in Social Villages, the other companies do. Experimental Enterprises and Innovation Enterprises leave the Planned Economy as soon as they are profitable in the market economy. Planned Enterprises are only found in Social Villages, but can also engage in foreign trade.

The aim of the work area of luxury supply is to enable the Social Villagers to achieve prosperity beyond basic supply, the form of which they decide themselves. Deviations from the principle of economic freedom are the Planned Enterprises, which also cover parts of the basic supply, but act primarily on the instructions of the plenary assemblies. Experimental Enterprises are completely free in their economic activities as long as they abide by the constitution. The same applies to Innovation Enterprises, which only have to market an innovation as a condition. People's Innovation Companies are established in structurally weak areas in order to provide jobs

---

[75] §210,1,2,5,6 Principles of economic order: BV Art. 94, KV Art.50

there.

10.1 Luxury supply policy

The Ministry of Planned Economy provides for the economic freedom of the Social Villagers through the work area of luxury supply, so that they can voluntarily be employees or entrepreneurs in addition to basic supply and can easily switch to other economic forms. As soon as the basic supply is secured, workers are allowed to work in the luxury supply work area. The money earned can be used for shopping in the social market, for saving or for additional consumption of goods and services in the basic supply work area.

Goods and services may only be exported to the market economy if the demand of the Planned Economy is met. Experimental Enterprises, Innovation Enterprises and People's Innovation Companies are exempt. The Ministry of Planned Economy may allow exceptions in the work area of luxury supply if imports have exceeded exports and a halt to imports would jeopardise basic supply.

The work area of luxury supply supports the Social Villagers with money on the one hand and with work experience as employees, founders, shareholders or employers on the other hand, as well as with in-service education, training and further education. Planned Enterprises, People's Innovation Companies, Experimental Enterprises and Innovation Enterprises offer various opportunities for this.

10.2 Equipment

State ownership is all means of production of all companies in the Planned Economy. Experimental Enterprises and Innovation Enterprises are usually different at each location and rarely span multiple locations. They are housed in multi-purpose factories and office buildings until they generate sufficient profits to survive in the market economy and then leave the Social Village.

Experimental Enterprises that have purchased production

inputs through the Start-up Fund can keep them after successfully exiting the Planned Economy. Means of production must be returned if the former Experimental Enterprise fails in the market economy and has to close, or pay back the monetary value if the former Experimental Enterprise is sold. The same applies to Innovation Enterprises that have purchased their means of production through the Innovation Fund. Planned Enterprises may only be sold if this does not endanger the demand of the Social Villagers and the foreign trade balance. The sale of Planned Enterprises must be approved by the whole people. The Ministry of Innovation is responsible for the conditions of sale of the People's Innovation Company.

10.3 Staff

To work in the companies of the Luxury Supply work area, Social Villagers must either submit an application, or they are recruited by companies, or they start an Experimental Enterprise or Innovation Enterprise themselves. All companies have a profile in the Labour Directory from the moment they are founded, as do all Social Villagers who are able to work.

10.3.1 Recruitment in the luxury supply

If you want to start a company in Planned Economy, you look for volunteers in the Social Village who want to join. To do this, profiles or groups can be created in the Social Directory and there is a notice board at the town hall. The Ministry of Media Affairs digitises the notice board daily and uploads the content to the Social Directory homepage. Free advertising is available on the Planned Economy radio and TV channel. Social Villagers have the free election whether and where they want to be gainfully employed in the work area of luxury supply. Experimental Enterprises and Innovation Enterprises can hire as many workers as they want. They report all vacancies in the Labour Directory. Planned Enterprises report all vacancies in the Social Directory. They may only advertise vacancies if the Company Auditing Agency's economic auditors certify the economic need for the vacancy.[76] People's Innovation Companies located in Social Villages give preference to hiring Social Villagers if they have the same qualifications.

10.3.2 Applicants

Via the Social Directory, all available jobs listed in the Social Directory and Labour Directory are automatically connected to the sufficiently qualified workers. As soon as the algorithm finds a match between the wishes of the employer and the employee, a corresponding proposal is made to both. If the proposal is accepted, an application or recruitment form is automatically created, which can be processed and sent off. This eliminates the need for paper applications. Otherwise, applications are made verbally. The Social Villagers visit the luxury supply workplaces and ask if there is a vacancy. If the desired job is in another Social Village, this can be done by telephone.

10.3.3 Dismissal of workers

One is dismissed from a Planned Enterprise if one shows less work performance, the Planned Enterprise has to reduce its production or the Planned Enterprise is closed. Experimental Enterprises and Innovation Enterprises can dismiss employees as soon as the enterprise owners demand it. If you are a shareholder, you must be paid out; if you are a majority shareholder, you cannot be dismissed. You will be dismissed from a People's Innovation Company as soon as your work performance decreases, the People's Innovation Company is closed or if the People's Innovation Company has fewer orders.

76Ministry of Labour - 20.7.3.6.2.1 Examination of the need for workers in luxury supply

10.4 Income in luxury supply

Those who go to work in the luxury supply work area to earn money have five options. Firstly, one can work in a Planned Enterprise and receive a monthly profit share, which is quite constant due to permanent supply contracts. Second, one can start or be employed in Experimental Enterprises and Innovation Enterprises and hope to make profits, be involved or become a shareholder if successful. Third, one can work in People's Innovation Company and receive a monthly wage under a collective labour agreement. Fourth, one can invent and market innovations and success models. Fifth, one can invest one's savings in the People's Stock Exchange to earn returns.

10.4.1 Profit sharing

Profit sharing depends on whether and how much foreign exchange has been taken in as profits. This profit is distributed proportionately among the jobs that generate the profits of a company. For this purpose, wage negotiations on profit sharing are conducted in a company committee[77] and thus replace collective bargaining.

10.4.1.1 Wage negotiations

Profit-sharing is paid as a wage for the respective job. Since different jobs require different levels of difficulty and skill, the wage for many jobs is different. Accordingly, the profit sharing is different for many jobs. If the wage is to be negotiated as a share of the profit sharing, a company committee must be convened. This requires at least 50% of the affected employees. Employees vote on the amount of wages once a year in a company committee when the Company Auditing Agency[78] audits are completed and all necessary data is available. In this voting meeting, it is announced how much has been taken and who has earned how much. All employees participate in

77 Ministry of Labour - 20.7.7.3 Company committee
78 Ministry of Labour - 20.8 Audit

the democratic wage negotiations. In the initial vote, everyone can state what percentage of the profits they think they will earn. Afterwards, it is discussed, argued and finally jointly determined which job has how much responsibility and what the workload is. What educational qualification is necessary for a job is determined by the Company Auditing Agency's economic auditors and determines the human capital factor that goes into the calculations.[79] The more necessary a qualification is, the more responsibility one bears and the higher the workload, the greater the share of profits.

If a person feels unfairly involved, they can report this as an unfair working condition to the Company Auditing Agency's economic auditors in their questionnaire. If the auditor recognises an unfair shareholding, a fair shareholding must be refunded retroactively.[80]

10.4.1.2 Bonus

The bonus depends on the performance of the worker. Every human fills a job differently. Those who make a special effort, are particularly fast, innovative, error-free or independent are to be rewarded for this. Those who have to do an additional project or exceptional extra work also receive the bonus. On the other hand, whoever takes over the work of another workplace receives the profit-sharing bonus of the workplace whose work was taken over on a pro rata basis for the period of time during which the work was taken over.

How much a bonus is depends on what percentage of profits is earmarked for bonuses. In a Planned Enterprise, the salary varies by up to 10%, so it is possible to earn 90% or 100%. Accordingly, there is up to 5% bonus and 5% malus. In Experimental Enterprises and Innovation Enterprises, the founders themselves can determine whether there should be bonuses. In People's Innovation Company, the bonus-malus system applies to state enterprises.[81]

---

79 Ministry of Labour - 20.7.3.6.2.2 Measurement of currency Working hours
80 Ministry of Labour - 20.7.3.6.2.5 Audit of profit sharing
81 Ministry of Labour - 4.8.2 Bonus-malus system

10.4.2 Licences for innovations

Innovation means increasing productivity in a workplace by changing work processes or using new tools. Employees who improve their workplace through their own innovation get a bonus as long as their workflow or tool is used. Innovations can also be inventions of individual Social Villagers. The innovation auditors of the Company Auditing Agency check and certify the innovation notarially and deposit it in the Ideas Directory or the Innovation Database at the request of the inventors.[82] The company pays the inventor 40% of the additional profits generated by the innovation. The innovation auditors carry out the corresponding measurements in the annual audit of the Company Auditing Agency. If other companies want to and are allowed to implement the innovation, they must pay a licence fee to the inventor.

10.4.3 Licences for success models

The auditors of the Company Auditing Agency check whether an innovation, a proven way of working or a popular product can become a success model. If the innovation, method or product is suitable, the economic auditor creates a profile of it in the Success Model Directory.[83] If companies from other economic forms implement the success model, they must give 5% of the resulting profit increase to the developer of the success model. The Company Auditing Agency, together with the auditors for business and innovation, arranges for the registration of an appropriate industrial property right, be it a patent, an entry in the Innovation Database or in the Success Model Directory.[84] The companies of the Planned Economy basically share all success models with each other free of charge.

82Ministry of Labour - 20.7.5 Innovation auditor, Ministry of Innovation - 9.7 Innovation Database, 8 Ideas Directory
83Ministry of Labour - 20.9 Success Model Directory, 20.7.3 Economic Auditor, 20.7.3.5.11 Marketing of Success Models
84Ministry of Labour - 20.7.5 Innovation Auditor, 13.3.2 Innovation Database

10.5 Planned Enterprise

Planned Enterprises are hybrid companies because they are used in both work areas. Planned Enterprises supply the centres with consumer goods and the companies with inputs. Planned Enterprises specific to one industry are located in specialised locations. Planned Enterprises for agriculture, textiles, craftspersons and location-dependent large-scale industries are located at each location. The output of all Planned Enterprises is determined in the annual needs assessment of all Social Villagers.

On the one hand, by producing raw materials, tools, machines and other means of production, they help the companies in the basic supply work area to be supported by the Planned Enterprises. In this way, they take on the task of being a provider.

On the other hand, they produce goods outside the basic supply that the majority of Social Villagers have desired in the needs assessment or have imported en masse. Since the wishes are not particularly different from those of other humans, these goods can also be exported.

Planned Enterprises have the possibility to sell overproduction in the market economy and thereby earn foreign exchange. However, they may only sell to traders who have registered their trading company in the Social Market Economy. These traders are allowed to offer the goods on the world market.

Social Market Economy companies are allowed to give work orders to the Planned Enterprises during peak periods in order to fulfil all orders from their customers. The Planned Enterprises complete the work orders and receive foreign exchange from the Social Market Economy company in return.

10.5.1 Ownership of Planned Enterprises

Planned Enterprises are 50% owned by the workers currently working in them. The other 50% belongs to the taxpayers, if tax funds have been used. The voting right of the taxpayers is exercised by the Minister of Planned Economy, unless a People's

Committee claims the voting right. If the Planned Enterprise operates without tax subsidies, it belongs to the Ministry of Planned Economy and all Social Villagers are entitled to vote. The voting right of Social Villagers is exercised by the Minister of Planned Economy and his deputies in the town halls of the Social Villages until the Social Villagers demand it with a quorum of 30%. Ministers are liable for faults, as are workers in the companies. In Planned Enterprises, which are subject to secrecy, only employees, ministers and their deputies are entitled to vote. The people can only have an insight and influence there through a committee of enquiry.[85]

10.5.2 State orders[86]

Planned Enterprises are state-owned companies that exist primarily to meet demand in the Social Villages and from other ministries. They fulfil state orders approved by the Procurement Review Board of the Ministry of Labour. The Procurement Review Boards are staffed by the tax auditors of the Company Auditing Agency.[87]

Planned Enterprises fulfil state orders such as the production of industrial property rights, weapons or computer parts for People's Computers and voting computers. These orders from the ministries of security, justice and digital affairs are subject to secrecy and loyalty to make it more difficult for criminals to prepare for technology through industrial espionage. These orders may only be awarded to Planned Enterprises because only nationals work there and fences and gatekeepers prevent uncontrolled movement of people.[88]

Since in the event of war, the Social Villages become barracks and all Social Service vehicles are converted for combat use, the Planned Enterprises for arms production are located in the Social Villages.

---

85 Ministry of State Organisation - 12.5.2 Committee of enquiry
86 §223.4 Weapons and war material
87 Ministry of Labour – 20.7.1.3 Procurement Review Board
88 Ministry of Labour - 4 State enterprises

10.5.3 Foundation and closure

Planned Enterprises provide goods or services most commonly imported from the market economy or demanded in a needs assessment. The Ministry of Planned Economy establishes and closes Planned Enterprises depending on the demand for imports by the social market or by other companies in the Planned Economy. The first step is to establish Planned Enterprises that can produce goods or services with the highest amount of imports in the previous year. The Planned Enterprises with the lowest demand from the Planned Economy must be closed.

10.5.4 Privatisation

Planned Enterprises that provide goods or services whose market is saturated in the Planned Economy but still has profitable sales in the market economy are transferred to the employees as a community of owners. The company must then move out of the Social Village and continue to pay the corporate tax rate of the Planned Economy on its profits.

10.5.5 Machine tax

All production machines are national property and their wages are collected in the form of a machine tax. The tax is calculated by dividing the price of the product sold by the number of workers replaced by the machine. It goes into the Unconditional Basic Income for Social Villagers.

10.5.6 Flexible companies

Planned Enterprises are flexible companies that support enterprises in the work areas according to the number of inhabitants and the need for imports. Through these enterprises, either only the demand of the Planned Economy or also the demand of the Free Market Economy and Social Market Economy is satisfied. The supply of Planned

Economy always has priority. If the work area basic supply has to import goods and services from the market economy, Planned Enterprises have to earn the equivalent value of the imports through exports. The demand for labour is covered by compulsory working hours in the basic supply work area. If the provision of a good or service by the Planned Enterprise is more than 50% more expensive than in the market economy, an export-strong Planned Enterprise can be converted into a flexible enterprise. The flexible company is then scheduled to finance the goods or services from the Planned Economy through its exports in order to maintain the foreign trade balance.

10.5.7 Standard Planned Enterprise

Standard Planned Enterprises are Planned Enterprises that exist in every Social Village. Depending on the capacity utilisation due to demand, the workforce grows or shrinks. Their goods are offered in the planned and market economy, with Social Villagers having the right of first refusal.

10.5.7.1 Modernisation company

The Planned Enterprise for Modernisation procures modern work equipment and ensures cooperation with the caretaker's office and craftsmen's workshops in order to carry out modernisations. This service leads to increased productivity in the companies and regular maintenance of the buildings.
The Ministry of Planned Economy regularly invests 20% of the business taxes in the modernisation of the Social Villages. The Planned Enterprise for Modernisation seeks out innovative work tools worldwide and surveys Social Villagers on if and when modernisation is due. The surveys range from a new coat of paint on a home to a washing machine that can wash more faster while using the same or less energy. The key is to increase the productivity of a job or the durability, sustainability and efficiency of infrastructure and equipment. The surveys will also ask for proposals for products or types of manufacturing

to be used. The aim is for the money to be used for upgrades that affected Social Villagers feel are necessary because they have to live with what may be an outdated condition.

10.5.7.2 Clothing company

There is a clothing brand from each Social Village that has a uniform logo. The logo is rectangular and oblong. On the left side is a national flag and next to it is "Social Village" and below that "City". City is representative of the name of the city in or next to which the Social Village is located. The logo is on each garment, but does not necessarily have to be visible on the outside. The garments are always produced at the respective location, issued to Social Villagers in a factory shop and charged to the clothing quota on the Social Card. Garments are sold to visitors and traders via the visitor card.
The tailors of the sewing workshop have to produce a minimum number of garments in bulk and are bound to the majorities of the Social Villagers in the design. Majorities are found by holding fashion shows and voting on collections during plenary assemblies. Once the basic supply of clothes is secured, tailors are allowed to produce entirely free creations. The clothing company mainly uses old clothes that have not been picked up by the Social Villagers from the central warehouse as raw material. New textiles are supplied from a specialised Planned Enterprise.

10.5.7.2.1 Mass-produced goods

The design for mass-produced goods is determined jointly by all the tailors. They are obliged to hold opinion polls or fashion shows where the Social Villagers can have a say in their upcoming collections. Special attention is paid to the comfort, functionality and beauty of the clothes when it comes to the rating of worn clothes from past collections. The tailors then take over good and eliminate bad ratings.
The bulk supply covers the planned demand for clothing and is settled through the working hours of the basic supply. The basic

necessity quota includes an annual quantity of professional, sports, sleeping and leisure clothing. Garments that are not called for are offered in the market economy. Goods that are not in demand are redesigned, supplemented by old clothes if necessary, and offered in the coming collection. New goods may not be produced if demand is low. A stockpiling of 10% in excess capacity is permissible.

10.5.7.2.2 Own creations

Social Villagers, visitors and traders can buy the tailors' own creations and leftover mass-produced goods. Tailors are entitled to put their own logo on their own creations. Own creations that have not been sold in 2 years go into the stock of mass-produced goods, which can be called up via the clothing quota.
If there is strong demand from the market economy for certain garments, tailors are entitled to produce more of them through working hours in the luxury supply work area in order to earn foreign exchange and pay business taxes.

10.5.7.2.3 Export goods

If there is a demand in the market economy, clothing is exported. The basic supply must not be jeopardised. The Planned Enterprise becomes a flexible enterprise. Tailors who are successful with their creations can set up Experimental Enterprises and thus leave the Planned Economy. The clothes that are exported are considered advertising for the Planned Economy's design work and souvenirs. The Ministry of Planned Economy can regulate exports if too much labour or raw materials are tied up in that company and are lacking elsewhere.

10.5.7.3 Upgrading company[89]

All persons and companies produce waste, which in the case of private individuals is recorded as sunk costs in the cost of living and in the case of companies as depreciation in the balance sheet. The aim of this Planned Enterprise is to collect, valorise and reuse goods that are sunk or written off costs for individuals and companies. These goods are literally free because their costs have already sunk or been written off. The extraction of raw materials and the use of production steps are reduced and the environment is protected. As long as the benefit from repaired or upgraded goods is equivalent to new goods, the standard of living is increased because less labour, resources and money have to be spent to achieve the same benefit. The Planned Economy thus saves taxpayers' money to support the socially needy. Products that are not produced in the Planned Economy and would be too expensive as virgin goods for Social Villagers become available, albeit in limited quantities.

10.5.7.3.1 Collection

The upgrading company uses the vehicles of the Social Service's on-call service to collect old clothes and bulky waste from private individuals and companies. Before the rubbish collection arrives, Social Service trucks drive through the streets and search the bulky waste for usable items. Containers for old clothes and old electrical appliances are set up in the country, regularly emptied at collections and delivered to the central warehouse.

The municipalities undertake to collect bulky waste from private households and companies at least once a year on three consecutive days. Simultaneous dates throughout the country should be avoided because the Social Service does not have that many trucks. In a municipality, all private households and companies should put their bulky waste on the street at the same time on the first day so that everyone can help themselves to it. On the second day, the collectors

---

89§190.8 Environmental protection

of the Social Villages come and on the third day, the rubbish collectors come. All citizens are entitled to help themselves until the waste collection comes. Whoever has something in his hands first, it belongs to him. In case of equal time, a coin is tossed. The bulky waste days are to be held in dry weather. The appointments and locations are to be reported digitally to the Social Service via the intranet by synchronising the appointment calendars. The trips of the Planned Enterprise are coordinated with the trips of the waste collection so that the trucks of the Planned Enterprise are at the bulky waste before the waste collection and do not interfere with their work. The collection trips are carried out with a Planned Enterprise employee and basic supply workers. The employee is a good judge of what is usable. He should make sure that nothing valuable is left lying around or that nothing worthless is loaded. The bulky waste is checked for suitability and loaded even if it is repairable. Anything that the workers find and want to keep for themselves, they are allowed to keep. This makes this compulsory work more popular.

10.5.7.3.2 Trade

Upon arrival at the Social Village, all parts brought in are photographed, digitally catalogued and filed in the warehouse. All parts are categorised as either fit for purpose or in need of repair. The catalogue is available through the Social Directory on the upgrading company's intranet site. Each part is given a profile. Users can discuss the repair online, search for materials and instructions, and order if necessary.
All Social Villagers and companies in the work areas can order parts as soon as they are catalogued. Whoever orders first receives the desired part and can pick it up from the Social Service warehouse. If the order is received from another Social Village, the goods will be delivered on the Social Service's next transport run.

10.5.7.3.3 Repair

If the part is broken, the Social Villager can repair it himself in the workshop or he can have it repaired by the upgrading company. This service must be paid for either by a valid currency or by working hours. For example, the time the repairer spends in the workshop could be done by his client in the work area luxury supply and credited to the repairer's working hours account. The material costs can be earned through work in the luxury supply work area, but could also have to be paid in foreign currency due to the import of necessary spare parts.

Parts that are in stock for longer than 6 months are sold by the Planned Enterprise via intra- and internet mail order and are only repaired before the order is shipped. The delivery times are indicated accordingly. As a result, this Planned Enterprise earns foreign exchange from the market economy with free goods from the market economy, pays business taxes to the Ministry of Planned Economy and profit sharing to the employees.

10.6 Innovation Enterprise[90]

Innovation Enterprises are newly established companies of Social Villagers that aim to conquer the market economy with their goods or services. Innovation Enterprises provide goods or services that are innovative and for which there is a gap in the market economy or in certain areas of the market economy. The Innovation Agency[91] checks whether goods and services are innovative, the economic auditors check the market gap. After a successful audit, Innovation Enterprises can access the Innovation Fund to start up.[92] Innovation auditors and the Innovation Agency accompany Innovation Enterprises until they can make profits in the Social Market Economy or have to give up.[93]

If requested by a majority of the Social Villagers, the business

90§233,2c,2d Unemployment placement
91 Ministry of Innovation - 4 Innovation Agency
92 Ministry of Innovation - 9.11.1.1 Innovation Fund
93 Ministry of Labour - 20.7.3.6.2.3 Audit of Innovation Enterprises

consultants of the Company Auditing Agency[94] can advise an Innovation Enterprise. The consultancy costs are then borne by the Social Village. The innovation auditors can commission the business consultants to provide advice. The Innovation Enterprise has to pay off the consultancy costs as soon as it makes profits. The repayment is 5% of the profits until the amount is paid off. Innovation Enterprises can become People's Innovation Companies and then receive business consultancy as standard.

10.6.1 Foundation

The foundation must be initiated by at least one Social Villager. Workers or founding partners may only be Social Villagers. Skilled workers may be recruited from the market economy if there are no willing skilled workers in the Planned Economy. All employees receive a guaranteed profit-sharing and a take-over guarantee in case of success for the first 5 years of the enterprise.

The aim is for the founders to manage their companies themselves from the time they move into the market economy and to be able to do without the support of the Company Auditing Agency. Whether there is a demand for the new good or service is tested.[95] The business consultants have marketing plans ready, which the founders can use free of charge, but do not have to.[96]

10.6.2 Financing

Skilled workers, goods and services from the market economy can be obtained through the Labour Directory. Skilled labour and necessary imports from the market economy are financed through the Innovation Fund. Goods and services from the Planned Economy are granted on credit when demand is met

---

94 Ministry of Labour - 20.7.7.6 Consulting services
95 Ministry of Labour - 20.7.7.6.3 Market and Operations Analysis, 13.3 Innovation Marketing
96 Ministry of Labour - 20.7.7.6.5.1 Introduction of success models, Ministry of Innovation - 9.7 Innovation Database

in the Social Village. Innovation Enterprises have to pay 15% of their profits in addition to business taxes until the loan is 110% paid off.

The innovation auditors accompany the start-up phase and determine whether work is being done profitably and whether the company can sufficiently remunerate its workers in the long term.[97] They warn founders against unnecessary investments and have a vote on the withdrawal from the Innovation Fund when 10,000 Dollars or more are withdrawn. All company managers of companies that have paid into the fund in the past 5 years are entitled to vote.

10.6.3 Professionals

Innovation Enterprises can use a special function in their Labour Directory profile to search for skilled workers in the Social Villages and for goods produced by Planned Economy enterprises or companies. For this purpose, the Labour Directory accesses the Social Directory database.

In cooperation with the Ministry of Education, the innovation auditors can order knowledge transfer for individual employees if deficiencies in corporate governance become apparent.

10.6.4 Industrial property rights

The Innovation Agency takes care of name, trademark and patent rights. It advises founders on how best to protect trade secrets and innovations. The registration of national industrial property rights is free of charge for Innovation Enterprises. Only fees for applications abroad and extension fees for 20-year extensions are charged. Extension fees only apply once the Innovation Enterprise moves to the market economy. Costs of foreign Patent Offices are financed by the Innovation Fund during the start-up phase.

---

97 Ministry of Labour - 20.7.5.4 Promoting innovation

10.6.5 Demand test

The demand test consists of two phases. In the first phase, the economic auditors examine the business figures of the competitor companies in the market economy. The market for the Innovation Enterprise's good or service can be local, national or global in the market economy.

To simulate market entry, the Algoracle[98] accesses the Labour Directory database and the Ministries of Finance, Labour and Economy. In this way, a demand is estimated and a workload of competitors in the market in which the Innovation Enterprise wants to become active is determined. The dataset includes, for example, audit data from the most recent audits by the Company Auditing Agency in all competitor companies in the market. This classifies whether the competitor firms are stable in the market or have demand problems or are even making losses, or whether they could increase the cost of entry by engaging in a price war. From the Labour Directory it can be concluded how many workers and resources are consumed in the market. The tax revenue from value-added tax and business tax can be used to determine how customers' demand for the goods or services and competitors' demand for labour and materials is behaving. All this data enables the Innovation Enterprise, through the algorithm, to predict where which product will find sufficient sales. The statistical results are supplemented by the experience of the Company Auditing Agency staff, who advise the founders and help to read the statistical results. The founders are not allowed to see the company data of the individual entrepreneurs. They only receive macroeconomic evaluations of all the companies examined.

In the second phase, the founders conduct demand tests. The aim is to find out whether the population is interested and how much they are willing to pay. The results are used to determine target groups and prices. They receive additional support from the ministries for media and digital affairs. In the television formats[99] , the idea or marketing can be promoted at

---

98 Ministry of Digital Affairs - 15.3 Algoracle
99 Ministry of Media Affairs - 7.2.1.4 Crowdfunding of the Week, 10.1.3.4 Crowdfunding, 10.1.3.3 Think Tank, 13.2.4.3 Innovation Lab

any stage of the business start-up. Each Innovation Enterprise can expand the profile page in the Labour Directory into a website with sales opportunities. The source code of these intranet pages can be exported. In doing so, the website is translated into the current programming language of the Internet. The web space and domain of the website is financed by the Innovation Fund. The Ministry of Digital Affairs hosts the website until it is ready for the market.

Advertising is part of the demand test. Advertising on state television and the intranet is free of charge until profits are made. Advertising through other channels of the market economy, such as television, internet or billboards, are financed through the Innovation Fund. Advertising to target groups and customer orders in the online shop are statistically extrapolated to measure demand.

10.6.6 Innovation Fund

The Innovation Fund is run by the Ministry of Innovation. The amount of money a new Innovation Enterprise wants to take from the Innovation Fund is decided by the Innovation Auditors after auditing the new Innovation Enterprise.[100]

Innovation Enterprises that have moved to the market economy and are making profits there pay into the fund. Each of these companies must pay 5% of the profits into the fund every year in which it has made a profit. The amount is levied in addition to the business tax and immediately paid into the Innovation Fund by the Ministry of Finance.

The administration of the Innovation Fund is the Company Auditing Agency, which can ask depositors to vote on the payment of large sums. The Company Auditing Agency's innovation auditors can approve or cancel payments from the Innovation Fund.

If Innovation Enterprises fail, the Company Auditing Agency reports this to the Social Village Manager, who withdraws the operating licence. The Innovation Fund bears the losses.

---

100 Ministry of Labour - 20.7.5.4.1 Approval of funds from the Innovation Fund

10.6.7 Failure

Innovation Enterprises may also fail to reach market maturity. This is the case if they have not been able to generate profits after 3 years, find too few employees or if demand is low and the willingness to pay of the few demanders is too low. The innovation auditors stop payments from the Innovation Fund. If the Innovation Enterprise has no more funds of its own, it must announce insolvency and close down. All buildings and items are returned to the Social Service and put into storage or used elsewhere. The plenary assembly of a Social Village can accelerate or prevent failure. Social Villagers can decide to make space for a waiting Innovation Enterprise, reduce, discontinue or charge for Planned Economy goods and services to the Innovation Enterprise. Equally, however, it can be decided that the Innovation Enterprise should continue to produce for the Planned Economy and be transformed into a Planned Enterprise.

In the event of failure, the money in the Innovation Fund does not have to be returned. However, if acquisitions are saleable, they are sold and the proceeds go back into the Innovation Fund.

10.7 People's Innovation Companies[101]

The Ministry of Innovation is responsible for the People's Innovation Company.[102] They are preferably built in regions that have few jobs. If a residential area is to be built for the employees, it is built as a Social Village. The People's Innovation Company is then the largest employer in the work area of luxury supply in this Social Village.

People's Innovation Companies can also be built in existing Social Villages or up to 5 kilometres away, if the specialisation of the located planned or Innovation Enterprises fits well with the input factors of the People's Innovation Company. Missing supplier enterprises can be built as Planned Enterprises directly in the same Social Village. Suitable Innovation Enterprises

---

101 §154.4 Tax reduction
102 Ministry of Innovation - 10 People's Innovation Company

can be converted into a People's Innovation Company after approval by the owners and the Company Auditing Agency. People's Innovation Companies located in Social Villages prefer to hire Social Villagers, provided they are sufficiently skilled.

If the People's Innovation Company is privatised or closed down and there are redundancies, the former employees can stay where they live and look for new jobs in the luxury supply work area.

10.8 Experimental Enterprise[103]

Experimental Enterprises can be set up by one or more Social Villagers. Experimental Enterprises serve the purpose of testing business ideas. Anyone who has a business idea can publish it in the Social Directory and search for suitable employees. Or one can tell the business idea at the plenary assembly in order to be able to find employees and customers. In their free time, volunteers can then produce the first products or provide services, which they are allowed to sell in all economic forms to test demand. Experimental Enterprises can become Planned Enterprises.

10.8.1 Foundation

If enough voluntary Social Villagers are found to start the Experimental Enterprise, they report the Experimental Enterprise by creating a new profile in the Labour Directory. With the data entered, a simulation of the Algoracle[104] can be accessed immediately. In an automated message, the founders are invited to an appointment at the town hall to receive advice from Company Auditing Agency staff at the Ministry of Labour office. There, an investigation is carried out to determine whether the services of the Experimental Enterprise are in demand in the market economy but insufficiently offered. The Company Auditing Agency's economic auditors

---

103 §230,2e Social Security, §233,2c,2d,3 Unemployment Placement
104 Ministry of Digital Affairs - 15.3 Algoracle

check whether goods or services are inadequately offered, using the Company Auditing Agency's data records.[105] If opportunities arise here, the Experimental Enterprise can receive money from the Start-up Fund.

10.8.2 Start-up Fund[106]

All Experimental Enterprises can receive money from the Start-up Fund to set up a trial enterprise. The money is for the purchase of inputs. The founders place the orders with the Company Auditing Agency, which audits them. If the orders are economically necessary, they are procured and delivered. The purchase orders are taken from the Buyers' Association, the Company Auditing Agency's Purchasing Department or the Procurement Office.[107]

Experimental Enterprises that have received money from the Start-up Fund and are successful in the market economy must pay 3% of this into the Start-up Fund in each year in which they generate profits.

The initial endowment of the fund, is financed by a government bond. The Ministry of Planned Economy issues them on the People's Stock Exchange. The term ends as soon as successfully established companies have paid in 111% of the initial endowment. The Ministry of Planned Economy is allowed to gradually withdraw 111% of the value collected through bonds from the Start-up Fund. 1% goes to the Ministry of Planned Economy as profits and 110% to the bond buyers.

10.8.3 Resources

Founders of Experimental Enterprises can apply for operating funds from the Social Service. Operating funds are unused goods, rooms or buildings and the temporary use of the workshop. All funds beyond this must be raised by the founders themselves or financed through the Start-up Fund.

---

105 Ministry of Labour - 20.7.3 Economic auditor
106 §230,2e Social security, §233,3 Unemployment placement
107 Ministry of Labour - 20.7.7.5 Purchasing Department, 6 Procurement Office

Founders can use the Start-up Fund by submitting orders for working capital to the Company Auditing Agency office in the town hall. There, the orders are checked for their economic viability and ordered if necessary. Delivery is made via the Social Market or via the Social Service, provided that the orders can be provided by the Planned Economy. The primary objective is to use stock of the Planned Economy as working capital or to pay Planned Enterprises for their delivery of the orders with foreign exchange from the Start-up Fund. Only if certain performance characteristics cannot be met by the products of the Planned Economy, import from the Social Market Economy is permissible. If the necessary performance characteristics can only be found in the Free Market Economy, imports may also be made from there.

10.8.4 Location

Experimental Enterprises do not necessarily have to be located in the Social Village. Renting or buying real estate outside the Social Villages is not possible through the Start-up Fund. However, if one of the founders owns real estate or rents it from their own assets and only provides the operating funds via the Start-up Fund, this is possible. Otherwise, Experimental Enterprises are free to make their own election as to which Social Village they wish to establish themselves in. At their first appointment, the Company Auditing Agency advises the founders on which Social Villages would be most suitable for a start-up in terms of their specialisation or skilled labour.

10.8.5 Leaving the Planned Economy

As soon as the Experimental Enterprise makes profits, it must pay 40% business tax on them. As soon as the Experimental Enterprise has procured all the necessary resources, can cover its costs in the Social Market Economy, earns sufficient wages, has moved its business to the market economy and has started its work, the founders of the Experimental Enterprise, including the workers, must leave the Social Village within 12 months. For families, the rule is that moving out must take place after a maximum of 3 years of profit.

10.8.6 Failure

If an Experimental Enterprise cannot pay for the second supply of inputs or does not make profits sufficient to survive in the market economy after 3 years, it must close the Experimental Enterprise. Operating funds are returned to the Social Service or sold. The proceeds from the sale go into the Start-up Fund.

10.9 Research and development[108]

In the Social Village, residents conduct voluntary research in their free time, employees conduct research in companies and enterprises, and pupils and students conduct research in the Education Centre. Research enables Social Villagers to earn an income in the luxury supply work area in two ways.
Firstly, they can conduct research themselves. To do so, they can either pursue their research projects individually, complete research contracts from the Research Cost Fund[109] or join a research community of the Ministry of Education,[110] or the Planned Economy. The aim of research in the Social Village is to develop as many new industrial property rights as possible in a short time in order to provide additional income for the inventors and the state. All applications for industrial property rights are free of charge for Social Villagers. During the application process, inventors are accompanied by innovation auditors from the Company Auditing Agency. Through innovation companies, the readiness of an innovation for series production can be checked. For these services, the Ministry of Planned Economy receives 40% of the licence income or the proceeds from the sale of the industrial property right. If industrial property rights are suitable for the establishment of a People's Innovation Company, the Ministry of Innovation makes an offer to the inventor or inventors.

108§154.4 Tax reduction
109Ministry of Innovation - 5.3.1 Research Cost Fund
110Ministry of Education - 11.7.1 Research community

Secondly, Social Villagers can participate in studies. The Social Villages can be used as a testing ground for studies by private institutes from other economic forms. The prerequisite for this is that the Social Villagers agree and money is paid to the Ministry of Planned Economy and the Social Villagers for participation. Of the amount to be paid, 40% goes to the Ministry and 60% to the Social Villagers involved.

10.9.1 Research community

The Ministry of Planned Economy ensures that research projects can be carried out quickly and in a target group-oriented manner. To this end, research communities are formed to work together on a research project. Research communities can become part of the People's Innovation Company Think Tank[111] in order to conduct research freely, or they can join a research institute or subject area of a college.

In the colleges, research studies are prepared that are conducted with Social Villagers. Depending on which target group the research concerns, certain homes, schools and companies from the two work areas take part in the studies. To do this, they fill out questionnaires, carry out experimental protocols, build and test prototypes. Researchers and test persons work closely together, exchange information regularly, coordinate their work and share the data.

10.9.1.1 Researchers and test persons

The researchers and test persons can vote democratically on whether they want to participate in a research project or not. Depending on who is affected, residents, employees of one or more companies, learners of one or more subjects and year groups, and college students of one or more seminars, subject areas or institutes are involved. The Ministry of Planned Economy coordinates its approach with the Ministries of Innovation, Education and Labour.

---

111 Ministry of Innovation - 11 People's Innovation Company Think Tank

10.9.1.2 Size of research communities

Social Villages with their residents offer a good testing ground because all target groups are present separately and easy to find. Therefore, democratic participation of the target groups in the research projects is also possible, because they meet regularly anyway at the Sunday plenary assemblies. Residents, businesses, centres and companies in Planned Economy can participate in research communities, but so can all other volunteers. Depending on the nature of the research project, Planned Economy research communities can participate in a state research project and work in a state-wide alliance with educational institution research communities. The aim of large research communities is to research a project as quickly as possible, and Social Villages provide standardised testing conditions.

10.9.1.3 Request to the research community

A prerequisite for the request is that a profile is created for the idea in the Ideas Directory. This profile can then be added to the Social Directory, either to the profile of an existing research community or a new profile is created. Volunteer researchers can be advertised at plenary assemblies. Once a year, there is a plenary assembly to collect ideas. All ideas from the previous year are listed, rated and voted on. The final vote is about which research communities implement which ideas in research projects.

The research communities can be approached by any resident, employee, entrepreneur, pupil or college student of Planned Economy to implement an idea for a research project. If an idea does not receive a majority vote from researchers and test persons, it will not be carried out by the research community. If a majority is obtained, the research community can still be expanded. First, a sample is taken to see how the initial results went with a small group of people. Then the idea generator can apply to the Ministry of Planned Economy for a new voting on whether the research community should be expanded. All old and new persons affected are then eligible to vote.

The research community can be extended to the entire country. To this end, all schools, colleges, state institutes, Social Market Economy companies, People's Innovation Company think tanks and mobile Innovation Labs will be approached to see if they would like to participate in a research project.

10.9.2 Education and research

If graduates want to earn money with their thesis, they can choose research contracts from companies from the Research Cost Fund[112] that fit their specialist department. For this, they can also join a research community to get enough researchers and test persons. Research communities use educational institutions to conduct research within the framework of graded performance records.

The companies of the Planned Economy are allowed to have research projects carried out in the education centres or to set up cooperative ventures. In the co-operations, the company premises or company resources are used to carry out the practical research work. The teaching sites are used to conduct the theoretical lessons and may be visited by employees of the companies to instruct the students in their upcoming research work.

10.9.3 Research focus on biotechnology

The research focus of Planned Economy is biotechnology. The focus does not mean that no other research projects may be carried out. The focus means that biological and biotechnological processes can be researched in each Social Village and that additional weekly hours and equipment are provided for teaching in the Social Village Education Centres. The Minister for Planned Economy determines the research focus or has the people vote on it.

Animal and plant species are researched and their microbiological processes are reproduced, understood and replicated. The aim is to be able to produce raw materials of all

112 Ministry of Innovation - 5.3.1 Research Cost Fund

kinds through biological processes in the Social Village using biomass in laboratories and bioreactors. For example, steel is replaced by a stable bone substance that grows into the desired shape through genetic programming. Glue can be produced by re-growing a spider's gland.

The educational centres offer courses in which the knowledge of biotechnology is taught in all school forms in a building-up manner. Research papers are planned as final theses, and graduates are free to choose their field of research within biotechnology.

Each Social Village produces different types of biomass. The algae batteries in the fence make up the largest share, which is earmarked for research and production. As biotechnology is a broad field, Social Villages specialise in different areas. Each Social Village has a biomass reactor in the Energy Centre and a biomass reactor in the Education Centre. Research projects are coordinated in the Social Directory so that duplication can be avoided and research projects can be approached from several angles. Those interested in a particular form of biotechnology may have to move to study or work with it.

In the long term, Planned Economy thereby provides products that are supported by fuels that are available on earth for as long as humans can live on earth, because humans consume the same fuels. The raw materials for the products do not have to be imported, but can be extracted locally. All products are biodegradable, thereby reducing the cost of waste treatment.

10.9.4 Innovation workshops and laboratories

Innovation can mean repairing old, worn-out things and creating new or novel ones. For this purpose, there is at least one Innovation Workshop and Innovation Lab in each Social Village, run by the Ministry of Innovation.[113] If the workshop or lab is fully booked, there is a waiting list and the usage time for everyone is reduced to 60 minutes. To shorten the waiting time, one can offer one's help to the persons currently active in the workshop or lab to speed up their work. If the

113 Ministry of Innovation - 6.5 Mobile Innovation Labs, 9.3 Innovation Workshops

waiting time for the first person is one week, the capacities are exhausted and an expansion must take place.

All Social Villagers are allowed to use the Innovation Workshop. They are a supplement to the workshop, but do not replace it. Mostly, the Innovation Workshops are used as a first temporary production site where Innovation Enterprises produce prototypes and successful small series before they get their own working spaces. Inventors can also work in the innovation workshops and request workers from the luxury supply work area.

Each Social Village has various special tools in its innovation workshop, which can also be exchanged between the Social Villages. Each innovation workshop always has a 3D scanner and printer, a CNC milling machine, a laser, basins, ovens and specially lit and ventilated chambers as well as 4 programmable industrial robots together with the necessary computers and programmes to support these devices with data.

In order to create something new, all Social Villages have at least one permanent stationary Innovation Lab. It is equipped with laboratory facilities that the Social Villagers decide to use. All equipment that is not currently in use in the mobile Innovation Labs is stored and used in the Social Village laboratories. The use of the Innovation Labs is open to all Social Villagers and follows the same rules as the use of the mobile Innovation Labs. Due to the focus on biotechnology, each lab has the necessary facilities and equipment for biotechnological research. As an alternative room, the science classrooms of the Education Centre can be used after opening hours.

10.9.5 Research directions

The Social Villagers decide which research directions there are and to what extent they are pursued, either personally and voluntarily or jointly in a voting. Joint voting is always necessary when capacities are limited or when there is to be cooperation in a research community. In every Social Village, at least market research, basic research, operational research and business research is conducted.

10.9.5.1 Market research

Businesses, centres and companies regularly conduct surveys among employees and customers to record satisfaction with production methods, goods or services. In addition to the standardised questions with tick boxes, there are free fields for praise, criticism and proposals. The data obtained is reported to the Company Auditing Agency, which shares the results with the participants. The aim is to research the Planned Economy market as accurately as possible in order to limit surplus or shortage. Market research in the market economy is limited to measures included in the demand test for Innovation Enterprises.

10.9.5.2 Basic research

Residents and companies of the Social Villages can participate in basic research. Necessary steps that still need to be taken are published annually by the Social Village colleges for their specialist department. In this way, they provide Social Villagers with entry points where the Think Tank groups can start. Costs for research projects can be fully or partially covered by the Ministry of Innovation[114] . Within the framework of the People's Innovation Company Think Tank, rooms and materials are provided that are available in the Social Village and are envisaged as necessary in the research project.

10.9.5.3 Operational research

Employees who are new to a job are asked after 2, 4 and 16 weeks what they would do differently or which activities they think could be improved. The proposals are discussed with the team and introduced if efficiency can be improved. In companies, the affected team or staff votes on whether the proposals are implemented. In any case, all proposals are entered into the company's or the company's profile in the Innovation Database so that all other companies in the Planned Economy can access the proposals. Exceptions to

114Ministry of Innovation - 5.4.7 Basic research

this are ideas that are so innovative that they must first be registered as industrial property rights. This task is carried out by the innovation auditors of the Company Auditing Agency. Staff members who come to their workplace fresh from training or further education give one or more interactive presentations to the colleagues after 2 months. The content should be innovations that have not yet been implemented. The innovation auditors and legality auditors of the Company Auditing Agency check during the surveys in the course of the annual audit whether suggestions for improvement have been taken up and discussed and whether an attempt has been made to implement them.[115]

10.9.6 Studies and test persons

Researching companies, institutes and colleges can carry out studies in Social Villages for a fee and create laboratory conditions for themselves in the Social Village centres. Only studies that test what benefits humans, keeps them healthy or makes them healthier are permitted. Not permitted are means that test whether someone is harmed by something.
The Research Directory[116] lists all studies currently offered in the Social Village. There is also a link to the outcome of the study and today's research results. Test persons who have participated in the study can comment on how they are doing throughout their lives on the profile of the research project.

10.9.6.1 Laboratory conditions

Many influencing factors can be standardised in the Social Village, such as same food, same housing situation or same work. All living conditions follow the Planned Economy conditions and behaviour is mostly recorded through the social card. For example, one could participate in a study about food. At the food counter, there is food in a designated area that has been prepared based on criteria from the study.

---

115 Ministry of Labour - 20.7.6.10 Enforcement of innovation law
116 Ministry of Innovation - 5.3 Research Directory

Those who permanently follow the instructions of the study and only eat the marked dishes get money for it. Whether the test person adheres to the study guidelines can be tracked via the social card. If he does not adhere to them, his deviation can be used to make the standard deviation more precise. The money paid out for participation in the study decreases for each deviation.

10.9.6.2 Salary

Test persons participating in the study receive a salary in the work area of luxury supply. The amount is transferred from the researching companies, institutes or colleges to the Ministry of Planned Economy, where 40% is deducted in business tax and the rest is paid to the test persons on their social card.

10.9.6.3 Collaboration on studies

Studies of residents, companies, entrepreneurs and educational institutions in Planned Economy provide test persons with further opportunities. Test persons are asked at the beginning and end of the study whether they would like to cooperate in the evaluation. If they wish to cooperate, they can use the equipment in the Education Centre, Innovation Lab or workshops.

10.9.6.4 Self-study

Social Villagers who observe themselves or work and notice regularities that can be formulated into if-then or ever-then hypotheses can enter this in the Research Directory in a profile that is linked to their profile from the Persons, Education and Labour Directory. The observation must be described, tagged, sorted into categories and assigned to one or more sectors or subject areas. Research institutions can use the results of the self-studies and recruit the persons who have studied themselves as possible test persons.

11 Planned Economy economic sectors

All Social Villages offer basic supply sectors. In addition, each location specialises in at least one sector. Thus, appropriate education and training in specific subject areas can be provided in the Education Centre on a part-time basis. Necessary human capital and the promotion of raw materials are located at the same location.

11.1 Specialisation at the location

All locations specialise in labour services that their Planned Enterprises can best provide there. For example, Social Villages with large state-owned land holdings in the surrounding areas get to specialise in agriculture. Specialised Social Villages support all other Social Villages with their specialised goods. For example, only one Social Village has a factory for computers and supplies all other Social Villages.

Each location has the necessary educational qualifications in its specialist department. Unemployed people with suitable qualifications are preferred to find employment there and can continue to work in their specialist department. This may require a move. Where there is a shortage of skilled workers in a qualification, Social Villagers may be forced to move or commute. The compulsion must be determined by a plenary assembly. A majority of 50% in the Social Village of origin and the Social Village of destination applies. The decision to move or commute is up to the Social Villager. The Ministry of Planned Economy bears the travel or relocation costs.

People's Innovation Companies, Experimental Enterprises or Innovation Enterprises can set up in specialised locations in order to obtain goods and personnel more easily. In general, each company is free to choose the location in which it wants to open. Transport costs for goods or travel costs for service providers from the specialised locations must be borne by the companies themselves.

11.1.1 Construction

The industry covering the construction sector has locations with forestry areas, sawmills, quarries and factories for iron and steel, cement, hemp bricks, bricks, building materials and construction machinery. Here, Planned Enterprises produce finished building components that are assembled in the Social Villages using a modular system. These include all components of all buildings and fencing systems. In other Planned Enterprises, construction machinery is manufactured, ranging from cordless screwdrivers to crane trucks with concrete pumps. The construction industry is increasingly replacing iron, steel and cement with biotechnological substitutes.

11.1.2 Food

The industry that covers the food sector has locations with extensive fields, stables, greenhouse facilities, agri-factories, hunting and fishing areas. Here, large animals such as cattle and horses are raised in large herds, which are individually given as working animals to the Social Villages or slaughtered in the slaughterhouse. Dairy cows are kept in these Social Villages and dairies are run to support the Social Villages with dairy products. The agriculture here is also done with permaculture, where the animals take on a landscape maintenance task in the ecosystem and are eaten at the end of their lives.

11.1.3 Textiles

The industry covering the textile sector takes the wool from all the sheep flocks and all the harvested hemp plants from the Social Villages. The specialised Social Villages house Planned Enterprises such as weaving mills and sewing factories. In hemp production, care is taken to grow specific varieties of hemp according to the demand from the Social Villages and to grow specific varieties that are as versatile as possible. Hemp is used to produce textiles, cereals, building blocks, medicines and intoxicants. If the grain harvest threatens to be small, the hemp must flower out to form hemp nuts that are added to the grain harvest.

Petroleum-based synthetic fibres are made from recycled plastic. Biotechnology research is developing biodegradable synthetic fibres to replace petroleum-based products.

11.1.4 Health[117]

The industry covering the health sector is represented in each Social Village by the Health Centre, where research studies are always carried out on behalf of the university hospitals. In certain locations, there are university hospitals that specialise in researching medicines, training physicians and operating on or treating particular diseases. The pharmaceutical industry in Planned Economy is a collaboration between the specialities of health, electrical engineering, chemistry and biotechnology. Planned Enterprises produce generic drugs and conduct research in cooperation with the educational institutions of the Social Villages. New developments are brought to market and spun off into Innovation Enterprises. The Planned Economy specialises in research on the use of medicinal plants, which are grown in the Social Villages as part of the basic supply work area and prepared in the hospital pharmacy. This knowledge is shared with the Barter Economy hospitals.

11.1.5 Energy

The industry covering the energy sector is represented in each Social Village by the Energy Centre and maintains the renewable energy sources of each Social Village. In addition to this, there are wave and tidal power stations in the coastal Social Villages and pumped-storage power stations in the mountain Social Villages. The power plants are built and maintained by the local social village population. The water pipelines from the sea to the mountains are built, maintained and used by the Ministry of Infrastructure. Planned Economy also uses these pipelines and does not operate its own nationwide pipeline network. Facilities for generating and storing energy

---

117§236,9,10 Health care: KV Art.41, BV Art. 117a

at buildings are produced by Planned Enterprises for the Ministry of Infrastructure.

11.1.6 Electrotechnology

The industry, which covers the electrical and communications technology sector, has locations with production facilities for devices and programmes, as well as 3D animation studios and 3D printer halls. Companies in Planned Economy are allowed to order devices and programmes they need for production here. The People's Innovation Company Intranet also operates its production sites at the electrical technology locations.[118]

11.1.7 Metal

The industry covering the metals sector has locations with iron ore deposits, mines and blast furnaces. The locations supply iron, steel, aluminium, copper and other metals that can be mined inland to the basic supply and luxury supply work areas on order. In case of scarcity, priority is given to the basic supply work area. Steel may only be produced with hydrogen, not with carbon. Biotechnological substitutes are being researched for all metallic raw materials.

11.1.8 Chemistry

The industry covering the chemical sector has locations with mines and refineries. All the processing Planned Enterprises in the chemical and pharmaceutical industries are located at these sites and supply the other Social Villages. The Planned Enterprises produce detergents, dishwashing liquids and cleaning agents as well as other chemicals that are only processed into end products or used in production processes in the other Social Villages. If there is a shortage, at least the basic supply must be covered and the production possibilities expanded.

---

118 Ministry of Digital Affairs - 13 People's Innovation Company Intranet

11.1.9 Biotechnology

The branch covering the biotechnology sector has locations with archives for all seeds, cells, enzymes and nutrient solutions that can be propagated through breeding. Biotechnology is a focus of all schools in the Social Villages and offers the laboratories to amateur researchers outside class hours.

Algae batteries in the fences around all Social Villages can produce or implement different substances. Specialised Social Villages can pump the algae from the fences of other Social Villages and transport them to themselves for further processing by Planned Enterprises. The educational institutions of all Social Villages have an archive of algae species in their biology lab that Social Villagers can experiment with and test in the fence. For example, part of the fence is stocked with algae that can be used to produce bioplastics. The Planned Enterprise for bioplastics takes care of the organisation of harvesting, shipping and further processing. Depending on the type of demand, algae farms can also be installed in the sea at the Social Villages on the coasts.

11.1.10 Mineral resources[119]

The country's natural resources belong to the people and are therefore only exploited by Planned Enterprises that are under the democratic control of the people. Therefore, in addition to the Minister of Planned Economy, the people also elect the politician who is responsible for all Planned Enterprises for the exploitation of mineral resources.

It is not mandatory that a Social Village is also built at the location of a Planned Enterprise for mineral resources. The raw materials can also be transported to the nearest Social Village that specialises in further processing.

---

119 §220.5 Agriculture

12 Real estate sector

Planned Economy's Social Villages are a mix of centre park, barracks, hotel, school, university campus, hospital and factory. They are fenced-off areas with Planned Economy and municipal cohabitation.

Social Villages are the real estate sector of Planned Economy. They are built on land that belongs to the state or can be acquired cheaply. Preferably, these are old barracks, railway or motorway facilities, housing estates or industrial wastelands. The buildings and infrastructure are constructed and maintained with the help of the responsible ministries and the Social Villagers.

In order to stabilise the Planned Economy, all Social Villages act in a social network. Capacities are flexibly distributed, buildings are closed down or put into operation. Stabilising the Planned Economy also involves maintaining a permanent surplus of 10% of premises for living and working. Fluctuations of more or less inhabitants and more or less business start-ups are made possible by sufficient real estate.

12.1 Development plan of a Social Village

Every Social Village needs a basic necessity of building measures. The following description of the Social Village is intended as a guide. The layout is flexibly adapted to the local terrain.

12.1.1 Traffic routes

There is a car park for cars in front of the entrance at the gate. The entrance consists of a two-lane road leading into a crossing. At the level of the fence is a traffic island with a barrier for each direction of travel. On the right-hand side of the road is a pavement leading past the gate. The fence consists of algae batteries, is 2 metres high, 0.3 metres wide and extends 1 metre into the ground. Along the fence runs a lighted walkway and the ring road that goes once around the Social Village. At the crossing of the gate, one can turn right or left onto the ring road or straight ahead on the central road through the Social Village. These roads are open to motor vehicles, have two lanes and are lit. All other roads are reserved for pedestrians, cyclists or suppliers. Along all paths, fruit and nut trees are planted and street lamps are set up with rubbish bins hanging from them. In front of the buildings are parking spaces for bicycles and street lamps.

12.1.2 Housing and food

The shape of the streets allows them to be divided into a right and a left side.

On the left side are the residential buildings. Directly on the central road, from front to back, are the houses for asylum seekers, unmated persons and senior citizens. In the second row behind them are the houses for families and children. Senior citizens live close to the gate, next to them are the asylum seekers and in the centre of the Social Village live the unmated persons. Senior citizens live opposite the health centre. Families with children live away from the ring road and central road, which is frequented by motor vehicles to avoid danger and displacement. All residential houses have a garden area, of which each resident is allocated an equal area. Since family houses are occupied by more persons per room, the garden areas here are laid out more generously than in the case of the apartment buildings on the central road. On the left side, adjacent to the family and children's houses, are fields and a wooded area where children are allowed to build tree houses as they wish. Adjacent to the ring road are greenhouses, small animal farms and fish ponds.

12.1.3 Education and sport

Next to the residential houses along central street begin the houses of the educational institutions. On central street next to the unmated person's house is the college, next to it the comprehensive school. Behind the unmated person's house is the children's house, next to it the nursery school and the primary school next to the comprehensive school. Next to the primary and comprehensive school are 5 sports fields with different surfaces and a lake with a sandy beach. The rear T-junction is located on a large asphalted square and can be closed off during events, so that an asphalted area of about 6 football pitches can be used without restriction. The Social Villagers vote on its use.

12.1.4 Supply and work

On the right side are the utilities and behind that the economic use areas for companies. Next to the entrance is the gate, which is also the security centre and has custody cells. Then follows the town hall, health centre, utility centre, laundry, workshop and innovation workshop, next to it the market garden, community hall, fairground and at the end the T-junction. Behind the health centre is a park with rehabilitation facilities. Behind the town hall are office buildings for free occupancy. Behind the supply centre is the central warehouse, which extends to the ring road, where the motor pool has its garages. Behind the laundry are the craft workshops. Behind the workshops are workshops for free occupancy. The space between the workshops and the community hall is occupied by the market garden and the area up to the ring road is used for agriculture. Behind the fairground is the area for specialised Planned Enterprises of the location.

12.2 Tenancy[120]

The Ministry of Planned Economy regulates the possibilities for using real estate in Social Villages in the Tenancy Law and Home Ownership Law. Generally, all buildings and materials in the Social Village belong to the people. The people lend a place in their Social Villages to the willing or needy. Social Villagers live for rent. The cost of rent is covered by compulsory working hours in the basic supply work area. Everyone is obliged to take good care of the Social Village

---

120§227,1,2 Rental business: BV Art. 109

equipment. Businesses pay their rent by supplying products to the extent determined by the Social Villagers in the needs assessment. Companies in the work area of luxury supply pay the highest business taxes of all economic forms and thus also their rent.

For residents, the place of residence is changed when the status changes because the Social Village residences are divided according to the number of rooms in a flat. The statuses are child, single, single parent, couple, family and senior.

Children have the right to live with their family or to stay at the children's home as often as they want. They pay their rent by regularly attending the nursery school or schools.

From the age of majority, the statuses of single person, single parent, couple, family and senior citizen apply. The time for moving out of the family is decided jointly by minors and their parents, in case of emergency by the police. From the age of majority, Social Villagers have the right to move into their own flat, depending on their status.

The timing of a couple relationship, a family or divorce, is chosen by the Social Villagers themselves and thus also the timing of their move. The status of couple and family has no specific number of persons or gender affiliation.

The senior citizen's time is determined by age and fate. Those whose children have moved out can decide whether they want to move into the house for unmated persons, couples or senior citizens. The life of comparatively younger sprightly senior citizens in the house for senior citizens is linked to compulsory working hours in the elderly care of the basic supply work area. If senior citizens receive a pension, they have to pay 40% of it in taxes for rent and can use the rest to reduce or consume their number of compulsory hours. The conversion rate is the hourly minimum wage of the Social Market Economy.

12.3 Residential buildings

Apartment buildings consist of bathrooms, bedrooms and living rooms. When the occupancy rate is high, neighbours share bathrooms and living rooms in common areas. In order to be able to adapt the buildings flexibly, the residential houses are built like accommodation in barracks. There is a corridor in the middle with doors to the individual rooms on the right and left. At the end of the corridor is a window. For flexibility, there are prefabricated partition walls with doors that can be attached and removed.

For cost reasons, cooking and washing are not done in the residences, but in the canteen kitchen and the laundry. The exception is the children's house, in order to be able to prepare age-appropriate meals and wash care textiles.

12.3.1 Capacities

Each Social Village must maintain an excess housing capacity of 10% of the total population of the Social Village. The vacant space may be used, but must be equally cared for and be able to be vacated immediately if needed. Vacant rooms may be requested by any Social Villager. The Social Service is responsible for the appropriate management of space. Vacant rooms are first used to maintain the minimum of 10 hotel rooms. After that, clubs, residents of the house and lastly residents of other houses are served.

12.3.2 Alignment[121]

The residences are oriented towards the living conditions of the residents. On the one hand, this is to facilitate harmonious living together. On the other hand, these groups of people also have similar needs that can be met by the house community and state services.

12.3.3 House rules

Each house has its own house rules. As soon as a quorum of 50% of the residents is met, the house rules are revised in a house committee. The caretaker chairs the committee and moderates the negotiations. The house rules must include the care of the house inside and out so that it is also preserved for

---

121 §186.2 Peaceful separation

future generations.

12.3.4 Deviations

If individual houses are too large or there are too few residents of any of the above categories living in a Social Village, the following houses will be grouped together first: unmated persons and single parents, couples and families, senior citizens and asylum seekers.

If there is a lack of space until new housing can be completed, rooms are occupied by several persons. Asylum seekers and unmated persons move together first, followed by senior citizens and childless couples. The measures include converting living rooms into bedrooms and occupying bedrooms with up to 4 persons.

12.3.5 House of unmated persons

In the unmated person's house, persons live alone in one room and share the common rooms. The common rooms consist of bathrooms, toilets and living rooms. The Ministry of Family Affairs organises regular get-to-know-you meetings in the house, to which all residents are invited, and maintains a singles exchange in the Family Directory[122] with a section of all unmated persons in all Social Villages. In the educational institution, training is offered on what behaviour promotes getting to know each other or a long-lasting partnership.

12.3.6 House of single parents

In the single parents' house, persons live in at least two rooms that are connected by a door. If there are 2 or more children, an additional room is provided. All share the common rooms. Single parents are allowed to decide in voting with their children whether they want to enter into marriages of convenience or pursue alternative family styles.

---

122 Ministry of Family Affairs - 7.2 Family Directory

12.3.7 House of couples

In the couples' house, each couple has a bedroom and a living room. All share the common rooms. Couples are persons who have no children or whose children are already of age of majority and are therefore entitled to their own flat in the House of Couples. To live as a couple in the House of Couples, one must be partnered and childless.

12.3.8 House of families

In the House of Families, each family with up to two children has 3 rooms and a bathroom with toilet. If there are 2 more children, the family gets an extra room. The common rooms are the living room and playroom. Families are credited with one working hour per child per day in the basic supply work area. The family house is surrounded by garden areas, one for each family. The gardens are directly adjacent to the Leisure Centre.

12.3.9 House of senior citizens

There are twin rooms in the senior citizens' house. All share a bathroom and living room. Care cases are primarily supported by younger senior citizens, social service staff and, secondarily, by hospital staff, but live permanently in the House of the Elderly. The house has a peripheral location where it is as quiet as possible.

12.3.10 House of asylum seekers

In the asylum seekers' house there are bedrooms and a living room. The bedrooms are occupied by 4 beds. Everyone shares the common rooms. Asylum seekers mainly take on the night shifts and unpopular services, because you can only veto the more often you have already been assigned to services you did not like. Since asylum seekers only live in the Social Village for a short time, they never reach this number. They receive lessons at the Education Centre with an interpreter present. The lessons are tailored to learn the things that will improve the situation in the home country. For war refugees, they are taught how to build a house and start a business. Political refugees are taught how to set up an organisation, such as a labour union, party or club, and the principles of democratic action and the rule of law.

12.4 Hotel

The Social Village Hotel is the first reception point for new arrivals or visitors staying for several days. Anyone who indicates at the gate when entering the Social Village that they want to stay longer than one day in the Social Village will find shelter here.

The hotel is either an empty residential building or individual rooms in residential buildings that are empty. In Social Villages, 10% of the rooms used as living space must always be empty in order to be able to spontaneously accommodate unemployed people. Each Social Village decides for itself how to provide the 10% surplus housing. This can also be ensured by a hotel of sufficient size. For an expansion to increase capacity, all hotel guests who stay there for more than 2 months are used.

Each hotel guest receives a list of tasks that they must complete in order to be allowed to stay at the hotel. For the supply of towels, bed linen and hygiene items, the hotel guest is given admission to the video-monitored storage. The reception is located at the reception desk in the security centre. The hotel staff are social service workers. However, they only provide instruction in the necessary work and control the room after the stay and whether all materials provided have been returned. Each hotel guest uses either his or her social card or visitor card as a key. All basic supply services for the stay in the hotel are charged via the card. According to the services used, the hotel guest must complete working hours in the work area basic supply or luxury supply.

In the hotel, Social Villagers have the opportunity to prostitute themselves and book rooms by the hour. Prostitution is a company in the work area of luxury supply that can be paid in working hours or money from the market economy.

12.4.1 New arrivals

Newcomers usually stay in the hotel for a week until they have decided whether they want to move into the Social Village, which house they will live in, which jobs they are qualified for or whether they would prefer to move into another Social Village with other specialisations that are more in line with their preferences and qualifications.

12.4.2 Guests

Guests of Social Villagers may stay in their hosts' flats or in the hotel for the duration of the visit. Guests without relatives are considered visitors. Visitors and guests who use services in the Social Village must pay for them. The price is equal to the contribution towards expenses plus a 40% profit mark-up. Any currency with an internationally valid exchange rate is accepted.

12.4.3 Residents

Social Villagers may spend a few nights in the hotel for social reasons, such as quarrels. Any stay under a week is compensated with compulsory working hours. All room preparation work is done by the resident.

12.4.4 Visitors

If you are a visitor to the Social Village, you have to hand in your identity card at the gate and get it back when you leave. The maximum length of stay in the Social Village is agreed upon. First, the visitor names his or her desired period, then the social service worker checks the room occupancy in the Social Directory for this period. Bookings in advance are possible. If there are no rooms available, it is not possible to stay overnight in the Social Village. Visitors can stay in nearby hotels and commute from there to the Social Village. For this purpose, they are offered the Social Service's transport service for a fee, provided it has sufficient capacity. The capacity check is also done by entering the data into the Social Directory and the computer programme working in it. If the basic supply has sufficient capacity to support the visitors, they stay at the Social Village Hotel with all services for a fee. The caretakers organise the cleaning work.

13 Finance economy[123]

The Ministry of Planned Economy regulates participation in international, continental and national financial and currency policies affecting Planned Economy. The Minister of Planned Economy formulates the laws in voting with the Ministers of Finance, Foreign Afaairs and Market Economy and puts them to a vote of the people.

13.1 Currency policy[124]

The currency of all Social Villagers is their working time, which is exchanged through division of labour. All goods and services produced in the Planned Economy alone, without purchases or subsidies from the market economy, can be paid for through the work benefit account and the social card. Prices are determined by the labour required, how long it takes and what skills and means of production are necessary. The Company Auditing Agency's economic auditors collect the necessary data and forward it to the Note-issuing Bank so that the value of the digital currency can be calculated. Wages and prices are expressed in working hours and Social Market Economy currency to make conversion easier for Social Villagers. The flat rate for basic supply corresponds to the fulfilment of the duty roster in the previous month.

The national currency of the Social Market Economy is also valid as a means of payment in the Planned Economy. All

---

123§217 Banks and insurance companies: BV Art. 98
124§219.3b Central Bank and Currency Policy

prices are also quoted in the national currency so that visitors, guests and traders can make purchases. Foreign currency is earned, firstly, by guests and visitors purchasing services in the basic supply businesses and centres. Secondly, companies in the luxury supply work area trade with the domestic and foreign market economy. In this way, foreign exchange, i.e. currencies such as those of the Social Market Economy, the Free Market Economy or other international currencies are collected by Social Villagers or the Ministry of Planned Economy. These foreign currencies can be used to import goods and services from the market economy. This mechanism ensures that the Planned Economy's foreign trade balance is balanced or in surplus when foreign currency is saved.

13.2 Digital currency working hours[125]

The digital currency of Planned Economy is called working hours and is only valid on the social card as a means of payment. There are no banknotes, but digital time recording and a work benefit account. Card readers in the cash registers, time clocks and door locks measure time and use. The principle applies: "Time is money".

13.2.1 Value creation

Currency is created when work of a certain difficulty is performed in a given period of time. The benefits that arise from the work have a price that is based on the costs, i.e. the time, education, responsibility, difficulty and materials involved. These costs are automatically recorded by the social card readers for time clocks and cash registers and made available as a record to the Company Auditing Agency's economic auditors. They then check whether the expenditure of time or material for this service is justified and how decisive human capital is in this. The economic auditors report their procedures and results to the Note-issuing Bank. The Note-issuing Bank calculates the daily value of the currency using the annual audit data and

---

125§219.3b Central Bank and Currency Policy

the current data from the Social Cards for working time and labour output via the Social Directory. If the labour output per unit of time increases, the currency increases and one can afford more for less labour input and vice versa. With the help of needs assessment and the duty roster, shortages are avoided that occur when one can afford less despite the same amount of work. The currency of working hours ensures the circuit of production and consumption within the framework of the basic supply of housing, food, clothing, hygiene and health.

13.2.2 Money supply

According to the quantity equation of money, the quantity of money in circulation is equal to the prices of all sales. The money supply of the Planned Economy without foreign trade is equal to the available labour time and the education level of all Social Villagers. The cost of materials can again be divided into labour time and education level if Planned Enterprises provide raw materials and produce materials from them. The velocity of money circulation is the degree of division of labour, i.e. how quickly a service is rendered in return. In Planned Economy, this velocity is high because most services are not stored but called up immediately. It decreases with increasing leisure time. The price level corresponds to the time needed to fulfil the requirements of the needs assessment and the remaining free time. Rising prices result in less free time and vice versa. Transactions correspond to all labour services performed in the recorded working time and the consumption of all labour services recorded in the cash registers.

13.2.3 Exchange rate

The exchange rate is flexible and depends on the relative economic performance between two economic forms or countries. The Note-issuing Bank sets the exchange rates daily. The exchange rate of the digital currency fluctuates around the capacity utilisation and the related work that more or less Social Villagers perform. Since the Planned Economy is designed for sustainable long-term growth, the value of the currency increases slowly but steadily at the same pace as labour productivity per capita. The digital currency represents the value of the Planned Economy.

13.2.4 Exchange

Visitors, guests and Social Villagers can exchange cash for digital currency. The exchange of digital currency into cash is only possible to a limited extent for Social Villagers. There is a vending machine at the gate for the exchange. Only the national currency of the Social Market Economy and the Free Market Economy are available at the vending machine as a means of deposit or withdrawal. Foreign currencies or precious metals can be exchanged, deposited or withdrawn at the People's Bank branch in the security centre. Currency exchange is also possible via the account at People's Bank. The work benefit account is integrated into the account at People's Bank. This makes it possible to use the digital currency as a digital means of payment on the intranet when Planned Economy products are to be purchased. The exchange takes place automatically in the currency specified by the supplier.

13.2.4.1 Exchange for guests and visitors

Guests and visitors exchange a monetary currency for the digital currency. They can use the credit in digital currency to pay for everything in both work areas. If cash is to be spent on the purchase of goods and services in the Planned Economy, it must be exchanged for the digital currency of the Planned Economy and is credited to the social card. Payment is made in reverse order. The exchange is only possible for the duration of the stay in the Social Village. When leaving, the amount of money must be taken back or will be forfeited. This is to avoid investing money, which can lead to currency fluctuations.

13.2.4.2 Exchange for Social Villagers

Social Villagers can earn the digital currency by working in the work areas to spend in the Planned Economy. They cannot exchange this credit into a monetary currency. If they want to earn money in the Planned Economy, they have to work in companies in the Planned Economy that export their products to the market economy. If Social Villagers want to spend this money in the Planned Economy, they exchange it at the vending machine like guests and visitors. It is possible to newly exchange money, but only in the same amount as money was deposited. In this way, Social Villagers can give themselves credit, so to speak. For example, you can deposit 10 Dollars, spend them and then go to work until you have saved up the 10 Dollars in working hours and then withdraw 10 Dollars again. Only Social Villagers are entitled to exchange their entire assets into the digital currency.

However, there is a separation between the work area for basic supply and that for luxury supply for Social Villagers. Compulsory working hours only entitle to basic supply consumption. Voluntary working hours in luxury supply companies only allow for the corresponding consumption in luxury supply. Only working hours outside of compulsory working hours can be exchanged for a monetary currency. Consumption in luxury supply is subject to the prices set by the companies. Consumers get the corresponding amount of working hours debited from their work benefit account.

13.3 Financial services[126]

The People's Bank is the only authorised financial service provider of the Planned Economy. The investment of money within the framework of People's Bank's offers is left to the account holder and is not restricted. Those who live in a Social Village and wish to invest their money may only do so on the Ideas Stock Exchange or People's Stock Exchange[127] . Lending is not allowed in the Planned Economy. Only research, start-

---

126§218,5,6 State Bank
127Ministry of Finance - 11.8 People's Stock Exchange

ups or investments by companies receive outside capital through money from the Research Cost Fund, Start-up Fund or Innovation Fund.

13.4 Planned Economy joint-stock companies[128]

Experimental Enterprises and Innovation Enterprises can be set up or transformed as Planned Economy joint-stock companies and owned by all their employees. If they break even and leave the Planned Economy, the employees can sell their shares on the People's Stock Exchange or unanimously decide to take the company to international stock exchanges. In Planned Economy joint-stock companies, workers can either buy their share of shares with a fixed amount or work and be paid out in shares until the share is reached. All shares are divided proportionately among each job. Jobs that take more time, have more responsibility or require a higher educational qualification have larger shares. Exactly how the division is made, or whether each workplace receives an equal number of shares, is determined by a company committee. Those entitled to vote are the employees. If you leave the company, you are paid out and get your share back, depending on how much the company is worth at the time. If the company grows and creates jobs, more shares can be issued, if it shrinks, departing shareholders are paid out and the shares of that job are not newly issued.

13.5 Insurances

There is no insurance in the Planned Economy. All services that would otherwise be covered by insurance are either financed by the Planned Economy's taxes or are accommodated in the duty roster of the basic supply on a solidarity basis. The insurance law regulates which insurances may exist in the Planned Economy. Anyone moving into a Social Village can terminate or suspend their insurance policies. If he wants to continue them, all insurances must be taken out in the Social

---

128§216.3 Joint-stock companies: BV Art. 95

Market Economy. If the Social Villager is insured with other insurances, he can use a special right of cancellation and switch to similar insurances in the Social Market Economy. Insurances necessary for child support of property or companies in other economic forms and not offered in the Social Market Economy may continue. The proviso of all insurance benefits remains that the insurance premiums can be paid in the currency of a market economy. The Ministry of Labour offers Citizens' Insurance for switching insurance between economic forms.[129]

14 Agriculture

Organised private agriculture is practised in all Social Villages to meet total needs. All open spaces are cultivated with permaculture to harvest high yields all year round and produce biomass for the biogas plant.[130] All indoor spaces that are lit will have appropriate crops, and unlit indoor spaces will have mushrooms. The plants are run using the methods of indoor agribusiness.[131] Social Villages in urban locations in particular can set up agri-factories, even underground, to meet their basic food supply.

Depending on costs and surpluses, urban Social Villages can also be supported with food from rural Social Villages. In principle, however, Social Villages should be able to support themselves with food if necessary.

14.1 Usable space

The agricultural land in a Social Village is found in buildings, gardens, by the wayside, in the fence and in fields. Food and raw materials are grown there, which are in demand in the needs assessment. Social Villagers perform part of their compulsory working hours in care and harvesting.

As far as possible, all yields are to be delivered to the central warehouse or the canteen kitchen for processing and

129 Ministry of Labour - 10.2.4 Citizens' Insuranc
130 Ministry of Labour - 19.8.7 Nature-based agriculture: permaculture
131 Ministry of Labour - 19.8.8 Agriculture away from nature: Indoor agribusiness

consumption. Consumption is allowed, but trade is not. First, the basic supply of food and raw materials must be covered.

In the living and working spaces, plants are placed in favourable locations. For the living space, edible indoor plants are offered in the market garden, some of which are able to recycle waste. Mushrooms are grown in dark rooms. Suitable planting systems can be lent out at the central store.

All residential gardens have ridge beds, greenhouses or small animal pens. At least one of the three types of food production must be present in each garden. The minimum sizes of the usable areas are specified. The rest of the garden can be freely designed.

In and around the Social Village, plants are grown by the wayside, between buildings and in fields that humans and animals can eat. Fruit and nut trees line all paths and roads. Streams, ponds, lakes and rivers are used to breed fish and aquatic plants.

14.2 Training

Each Social Villager is credited with one day of training at the Education Centre from the subject "agriculture" as working hours in the work area basic supply when moving in. The training day must be completed within the first year and includes all the basics of permaculture. Gardeners deliver the lessons and are available throughout the year for advice on location, cultivation and cutting for the Social Villagers.

14.3 Genetic engineering

Artificial chemical fertilisation or treatment is prohibited in the freely accessible outdoor area, as is genetic modification. Genetically modified plants may only be offered for consumption in the Planned Economy with special permission from the plenary assembly of the respective Social Village.

In the greenhouses of the market garden, industrial genetic manipulation of animals and plants can be carried out in a shielded environment. As soon as studies on the compatibility for humans and nature have been confirmed, the industrially genetically manipulated products can be used, but not for the production of food. This release only takes place when no damage can be proven in long-term studies with animals.

14.4 Emergency supply

Emergency food supply is practised through an emergency plan. By following the emergency plan, each Social Village is able to support its population with sufficient food. For this purpose, the entire garden areas including the actually freely available land can be used and all open areas can be cultivated with permaculture. If these areas are not sufficient, an agrifactory is operated. The emergency supply can lead to the Social Villagers getting less meat and sun-ripened vegetables.

14.5 Market garden[132]

In the Planned Economy, the market garden is responsible for organising the agriculture. Social Villagers cultivate their own gardens and areas allocated to them in the Social Village. The gardener service supports them with advice, seeds and breeding animals. The market garden administers and controls the cultivation of all usable areas designated for basic supply. The market garden has craftsperson equipment to grow crops, fish and raise livestock in a field, garden, room or building. The market garden occupies spaces in the central warehouse for craft equipment, greenhouses, flower beds, small fields, stables for pigs, sheep, goats, chickens, rabbits and geese, and fish farms. The equipment is lent out to Social Villagers, who receive instruction in its handling at the beginning. The market garden has greenhouses and an outdoor area. Genetic engineering can be carried out in the greenhouses, on the one hand through targeted crossbreeding, on the other hand through industrial genetic manipulation. Animals, seeds, cuttings and seedlings are grown to be released or sown by the Social Villagers in a given place. In addition to all these

---

132§220,1b,1d,2 Agriculture: BV Art. 104, KV Art.51

small-growing plants, trees are grown in the nursery, which are planted by the wayside and in the fields in the Social Village.

14.5.1 Gardener service

There is a permanent gardener service that administers the market garden. He trains all the Social Villagers, gives them advice, allocates areas for them to cultivate with plants and animals and controls the cultivation and animal husbandry. The gardener service gives advice according to the rules of permaculture on how to fertilise ecologically or how and where to plant, cut and care for plants and which farm animals are suitable. Those who do regular working hours in the gardener service receive further training in the Education Centre, which is credited as working hours. The only trained workers in the market garden are also teachers in the Education Centre. All other gardener service workers are employed in the basic supply work area. At harvest time, the gardener service can request additional compulsory working hours.

14.5.2 Animal breeding

All animals come from the Social Village Animal Network, where breeding animals are exchanged. Chickens, geese and rabbits are bred in the gardens. The Social Villagers on duty tend the herds of pigs, sheep or goats. They lead them around the Social Village to keep vegetation short everywhere and eat fallen fruit. Residents can lend out farm animals to mow or dig up the lawn in their garden. Cattle and horses can be kept individually as draft and farm animals and come from the specialised Social Villages for food. Surplus farm animals are slaughtered in the commercial kitchen.

Edible fish are bred in the ponds, which are created as mirror surfaces for sun-loving plants. As many ponds as possible are connected via small streams. To power the stream, an existing stream can be used or it can be created through height differences and a solar-powered pump. Fish can also be bred in modules that can be connected to the algae batteries.

14.5.3 Plant breeding

In the market garden, useful plants and seeds are grown for the seed bank. Together with the gardener service, the Social Villagers plant or sow the plants and then care for and harvest them independently. The algae batteries are stocked with the necessary algae in voting with the centres for education and energy.

Plants necessary for the production of medicines are grown in voting with the health centre. If they are toxic to humans or animals and pose a danger to children, for example, they may only be grown in the market garden's greenhouse or under specified safety precautions.

14.5.3.1 Seed banks

The market garden's seed bank is also located in the central warehouse. It contains seeds of useful plants that are best adapted to the soil and weather in the area of the respective Social Village. These include plants for the production of food, medicines, intoxicants and products such as paper, textiles, plastics and the like. The different seed banks of all Social Villages specialise in seeds of exotic and ornamental plants, so that all seed banks in the alliance have all the seeds on earth. Social Villagers and Education Centres can order exotic seeds for research purposes or for indoor agribusiness. If the breeding is successful and the yield finds a demand in Planned Economy, the seeds are multiplied and distributed to the seed banks.

The gardener service ensures that seeds are regularly harvested in its growing areas to fill the seed bank. Seeds are distributed to all Social Villagers who use them for agriculture in their gardens. Advice is given on how, when and where best to plant the seed. Breeding videos for all seeds in the seed bank are stored in the Knowledge Directory. Social Villagers can lend out camera equipment and a cutting station for this purpose. Social Villagers who grow plants can also submit seeds to the seed bank. All breeders are encouraged to produce creative crosses that are more resistant. Successful new crosses are published in the Social Directory and the seed banks of the other Social Villages are supplied with the new seeds. The seed banks also maintain the list of breeding animals that can be ordered through the animal association and picked up at the seed bank.

14.5.3.2 Algae batteries

The algae batteries in the fence of the Social Villages are used to produce plastic or edible water plants. If the companies in the Social Village need hydrogen as an energy carrier, it can be produced by genetically modified algae or electrolysis. Part of the algae batteries is available to the Education Centre. Here, experiments with different types of algae and gases can be carried out as part of the lessons. Some of these batteries can also be used by researching Social Villagers. Depending on the workload of the industry, more or fewer algae batteries are released for research purposes. If there are too few algae batteries in total to meet industrial or research needs, products from coastal algae batteries are requested from specialised Social Villages.

14.5.3.3 Intoxicants

The market garden can also provide space for growing hops, coffee, marijuana, psychoactive mushrooms, poppies or cocaine if there is a sufficient supply of food. The seeds of these plants are also available in the seed bank and can be grown as houseplants. In order to comply with the purity law for intoxicants, all purchasable intoxicants are prepared in the commercial kitchen. The purity requirement is checked by the pharmacist of the Social Village before the intoxicants are sold in the pharmacy. Devices for the production of alcoholic beverages, coffee, cannabis, cocaine, psychoactive mushrooms or other natural intoxicants can be lent out at the central warehouse. The production of natural intoxicants in the houses is permitted, but can be prohibited by the majority of the house residents. Cultivation in a greenhouse in one's own garden remains permissible. Yields can be consumed by the residents themselves or delivered to the canteen kitchen.

On the other hand, those who consume intoxicants in the Planned Economy that they did not buy are not covered by health insurance. Those who buy drugs in the Planned Economy as Social Villagers pay for the treatment costs of drug use in the health centre through a price surcharge. This replaces the Addictive drugs Health Insurance with a pay-as-you-go system of working hours. Anyone who buys drugs in the Planned Economy as a visitor or guest pays a surcharge into the Addictive drugs Health Insurance.[133]

Each health centre offers rooms and appointments for self-help circles, which are regularly visited by physicians or therapists for counselling purposes. Video instructions from the Knowledge Directory guide addicts on what daily routines they need to master in their collective self-therapy in order to be weaned from addiction.

15 Foreign trade[134]

The Ministry of Planned Economy regulates foreign trade law for the two work areas. Foreign trade deficits with foreigners are prohibited. The value of goods and services imported into the Planned Economy must not exceed the value of products exported. If something is to be paid for in the currency of another economic form or another country, sufficient foreign exchange must be available for this purpose. Foreign exchange is all internationally tradable currencies.

Exports abroad are only permitted if the needs of the Planned Economy are met. Trade relations with foreign countries must be legally secured by trade agreements. In the negotiation of trade contracts between the Planned Economy and the foreign economy, the affected Social Villages are involved through the plenary assembly. If foreign trade affects all Social Villages, the Minister for Planned Economy convenes a committee where all Social Villagers are entitled to vote and jointly negotiate the trade agreement. If foreign trade regulations affect the whole country, the ministries of labour, economy, finance and

---

133 Ministry of Health - 5.12.3 Addictive drugs Health Insurance
134 §225,4,7 Foreign Economic Policy

foreign affairs are involved. The Ministry of Foreign Affairs convenes a People's Committee to negotiate the trade treaty with the affected peoples.

15.1 Continental social policy

Unemployed citizens from an International Union member state can receive social benefits in Planned Economy if their unemployment insurance participates in the Continental Social Fund or the member state has paid in sufficient per capita.

Disabled citizens from an International Union member state receive social benefits in the Planned Economy if their member state has paid sufficient per capita into the continental assistance fund for the most disadvantaged persons.

Citizens from an International Union Member State without sufficient pension can live in the Planned Economy if their monthly pension is sufficient to pay for the development of the existing infrastructure.

The Ministries of Foreigners and Planned Economy ensure legislation to guarantee continental social rights in domestic Social Villages. The Ministries of Planned Economy or Social Policy of all Member States shall ensure the coordination of social law systems until the same laws on social policy apply in all Member States and a continental minister for Planned Economy can be elected.[135]

16 Tax policy

The tax policy of the Planned Economy is closely connected to its financial policy. The budget of the Planned Economy is derived from the working hours of the Social Villagers, business taxes collected, revenues from visitors and exports, value added taxes on imports, compensation from the market economy, and funds for innovation and business start-ups.

All tax revenue collected by the Ministry of Planned Economy is first used to cover the expenses of the other ministries for the centres in the Social Villages. The rest of the tax revenue

135 Ministry of Foreign Affairs - 5 Communitarisation, 6 Continental Policy

goes to the Ministry of Finance. The people decide on the distribution of all tax money in the budget vote.[136]
The Social Villagers also have the opportunity to generate profits themselves through their Planned Businesses and Planned Enterprises. In a budget committee, they can decide on the distribution of these funds.

16.1 Business taxes[137]

All companies pay business tax, which is only due when profits are earned from foreign currency collected. Experimental Enterprises and Innovation Enterprises do not have to pay business taxes in the first year. Taxes are managed through the People's Bank Tax Account to the Ministry of Finance. The tax rate can be changed by the Minister of Planned Economy in voting with all Social Villagers. The people have a right to object through a veto quorum.

Profit taxes are levied on goods and services shipped out of the Planned Economy into the market economy. The business taxes of the Planned Economy are 40%. They are supposed to be sufficient to generate an overall budget surplus of no more than 10%, in addition to value added tax and fees. If the surplus falls to 0%, business taxes are increased; if it rises above 10%, they are reduced, but only in the following year. This economic policy coordination is done in cooperation with the Company Auditing Agency and implemented together with the Social Villagers as part of the needs assessment.

16.2 Budget Committee

The Budget Committee serves to enable Social Villagers to use their self-generated profits for the common good in their community. Profits from the sale of Planned Businesses and Planned Enterprises go 50% to the Social Village where they were generated and 50% to the Ministry of Planned Economy. The Ministry of Planned Economy's expenditure is democratically negotiated with all Social Villagers in the

136Ministry of Finance - 9.5 Budget vote
137§150,1,3b,4 Business taxes

annual Budget Committee. Social Village expenditure is negotiated at a municipal budget committee during the plenary assembly. The budget committee applies to Planned Economy only and is held in parallel with the Ministry of Finance's budget vote, but is limited to the Ministry's Planned Economy funds. Expenditures may not exceed revenues; on the contrary, 10% must be saved. Savings can be released in case of losses or large investments by a committee in which all Social Villagers are entitled to vote.

In the final vote, the Social Villagers decide how much of the available assets should be used for needs assessment in the coming year for goods and services, invested in technical progress or saved for projects.

Funds whose money is earmarked are exempt from the provisions of the budget committee. However, Social Villagers can lodge an appeal against a disbursement via a veto quorum. The assets from the Innovation Fund may only be used to import new innovations or to make Innovation Enterprises ready for the market. The amount of money a new Innovation Enterprise wishes to withdraw is decided by the Company Auditing Agency after auditing the new Innovation Enterprise. The assets from the Start-up Fund may only be used to establish Experimental Enterprises. The Company Auditing Agency checks whether and where the Experimental Enterprise has a chance of success and releases the amount of money from the Start-up Fund that has been calculated as sufficient.

16.3 Financing of social welfare[138]

Social welfare is financed in five ways. In the first type, all Social Villagers develop the basic supply. In the second type, all volunteers develop the luxury supply. In the third type, Social Villagers develop excess capacity and export the excess supply for profits. In the fourth type, the ministries of Social Market Economy and Free Market Economy provide compensation. In the fifth type, business taxes and value added tax increase by the same percentage.

138§230,1,3-5 Social security: BV Art. 112, §130,2,3 Cultural protection areas and economic zones: BV Art.50

However, Social Villages are not only for social welfare, but nationals can also live there voluntarily. If the Planned Economy grows on its own because there is a surplus of births, many want to continue to stay in the Social Village or new residents move in voluntarily, then the Ministry of Planned Economy bears the costs of expanding Social Villages for these new residents.

16.3.1 Development of basic supply

All Social Villagers do compulsory work to generate the basic supply for all Social Villagers. This saves costs for goods and services for basic needs such as food, clothing, hygiene, housing, sports and health.

The compulsory working hours in the work area of basic supply provide staff free of charge. The staff produce goods with the help of community-owned inputs and offer services. If there are not enough skilled workers who want to live in the Social Village, they are bought in and receive wages in the currency of the Social Market Economy as state employees. The revenues of the foreign currency from the Social Market Economy come from tax revenues of the companies. To avoid such extra work, Social Villagers take further training in their compulsory working hours to be able to replace the skilled workers.

The operating resources represent costs if they have to be purchased. Through specialisation by sector, Planned Economy produces as many inputs as possible for basic supply itself.

16.3.2 Development of luxury supply

All Social Villagers can work voluntarily in order to load money onto their social card. With the working hours from the luxury supply, they can afford luxury goods from Planned Economy production. With the profit sharing they can afford imports from the market economy. If they work in Planned Businesses and Planned Enterprises outside compulsory working hours, they earn profits that they can distribute in the budget vote to treat themselves to something for their community. Experimental Enterprise start-ups are self-financing through the Start-up Fund, which provides them with seed money. The Ministry of Innovation is responsible for funding the Innovation Enterprises by operating the Innovation Fund.

16.3.3 Excess capacity

To avoid fluctuations in business taxes, all Social Villages have an overcapacity of housing and jobs of 10%. This means either Social Villagers have more housing and more to do or less housing and less to do. Only when the capacity is completely exhausted, or when over 5 years the overcapacity falls below the prescribed 10%, will the Social Village be expanded.

The Planned Economy prevents shortages by producing an excess supply of 10% from Planned Enterprises, which may be sold outside the Planned Economy. This sale must be reduced to the same extent as the demand in the Social Villages increases. This buffer gives suppliers time to adjust to an increase in demand. As long as there is no shortage and sufficient raw materials are growing, saleable surplus capacity can be built up in both work areas. The aim is to lower prices for Social Villagers and to actually be able to sell surpluses in the Social Market Economy and Free Market Economy or, if necessary, on the world market. Export will only be allowed if the profit margin is above 20%. Otherwise, these surplus capacities are reduced again to 10%.

16.3.4 Compensation payments[139]

The Ministries of Social Market Economy and Free Market Economy, which do not support the unemployed and humans in social need, have to make compensation payments. In return, they pay a per capita amount to the Ministry of Planned Economy, which covers the cost of expanding capacity in the

---

139 §45.4 Welfare state

Social Village.

Anyone who has become unemployed must state the company and in which economic form they were previously employed when moving in. This information is used for statistical cost recording. If an economic form or several economic forms produce so many unemployed people that Social Villages have to be enlarged, then the costs are borne as temporary tax increases by the ministries of economy affected. For example, if someone from the Free Market Economy does not find a job in the Social Market Economy or Free Market Economy, the Ministry of Free Market Economy has to bear the cost per capita. If a citizen runs different companies in different economic forms, the decisive factor is which company has brought in the most income for the currently unemployed citizen in the past 5 years. Depending on whether this was a Social Market Economy or Free Market Economy company, the Ministry of Social Market Economy or Free Market Economy is liable to pay.

The shares of the costs are calculated as a percentage of the number of persons who have moved into the Social Village as unemployed from the respective economic form. For example, if 25% of the unemployed come from the Social Market Economy and 75% from the Free Market Economy, then the Ministry of Free Market Economy must increase its taxes in such a way that 75% of the expansion costs of the Social Villages are covered within 12 months. The affected Ministry of Economy is responsible for the duration and percentage of the tax increase. The use of the ministry's own funds for Planned Economy to stretch the time over 12 months is permissible. The tax increases must not generate more tax money than was needed for the expansion. If there are surpluses, they must be returned to the ministries for market economy.

16.3.5 Tax increases

As a last resort, tax money can be used to finance it, shared between companies and consumers. Business taxes and value added tax are increased by the same percentage. The amount of tax increases depends on the amount needed and can be approved or rejected in the following budget vote. If all Social Villages are overloaded, a Tax-funded extension of services or Fee-funded services must be negotiated with the people in a committee. Once the Unconditional Basic Income is sufficient, a residence fee is levied in Social Villages to replace the tax increases.

17 Social policy[140]

The Ministry of Planned Economy is responsible for the operation of the welfare state. Under the welfare state, a minimum level of social security is provided to all nationals. Nationals in social need due to old age, disability, illness, accident, unemployment, homelessness, maternity, loneliness, orphanhood and widowhood are guaranteed admission to the welfare state.

The welfare state includes health care, promotion and protection of families and children, work for subsistence, food and housing, free education, research, development, business creation, information and self-management. The welfare state is provided in the Social Villages and is organised on a Planned Economy basis to be self-financing without subsidies. Grants are only required from the ministries of Social Market Economy and Free Market Economy if they provide strong influx through unemployment. State social benefits are limited to benefits in kind. All these services are provided in the Social Villages and offered in cooperation with other ministries.

17.1 Social welfare[141]

Social welfare consists of state services provided in the Social Village. Nationals have the right to receive welfare state services in the Social Villages. These services can be provided at one, several or regular appointments for So-called social commuters. An example is an appointment to take in a child for three nights because an exceptional emergency situation is plaguing the parents. Multiple appointments would be

---

140 §9.2 Right to assistance in emergencies: BV Art.12, §45 Welfare state: BV Art.41

141 §44 Social welfare: KV Art.38, §232,3 Occupational benefit scheme

necessary for example in the case of further education at school. Regular appointments mean moving in to the Social Village, for example, to pursue a degree or start an innovative company. Social commuters use the existing service facilities, which can more or less easily cope with 10% clients per day. In return, Social Commuters take over holiday replacements for Social Villagers.

A lasting service is provided by all residents of each Social Village to their fellow residents in a village community that offers housing, work and social contacts. The residents care for a lively neighbourhood with discussion groups, music and singing groups, sporting or cultural clubs and festivals in the buildings, streets or the fairground.

Social fraud can result from untaxed assets or unauthorised admission to social benefits. If there is suspicion of social fraud[142] , the police can be notified. This is announced in advance. This way, the suspected social fraudster can still make a statement and pay for the operation if he has the necessary money after all. Otherwise, the police will initiate an investigation into suspected social fraud.

17.2 Social emergency call[143]

The Social Emergency Call is an on-call service of the Social Service and is stationed at the gate in every Social Village. The Social Emergency Service is responsible for providing initial social welfare to nationals who are in social distress. This means short-term or long-term evacuation from the social environment. The Social Service mainly provides transport for social commuters or relocation for moving in and out. Anyone who is in social distress can contact the social emergency service via the telephone number 113 as well as on the internet and intranet. All those who report for this service receive radio alarms when they are needed immediately. There is a Social Service Worker and a Police Officer or People's Protection Service Worker at the helpline 24 hours a day, 7 days a week. The social service worker manages the telephone

---

142 Ministry of Justice - 8.16.2 Social fraud
143 §233.4 Unemployment placement

and the websites for the social emergency call. If a call for help is received, an emergency vehicle from the People's Protection Service[144] is sent to the person. If the person is unable to get to the nearest Social Village themselves due to the emergency, they are taken there. Either the People's Protection Service takes the person to the Social Village or the Social Service sends an emergency vehicle to pick up the person. Regardless of whether the person is brought or presents himself at the gate, he can stay in the Social Village hotel for a maximum of 7 days and receive psychological or practical social counselling. In the course of the counselling, it is decided whether a move to the Social Village is recommended, whether individual appointments for training, advice or therapy are sufficient or whether no further help is needed. Similar to a hospital, the Social Villages provide shelter for the time needed to regenerate human assets. The social emergency service brings together people seeking help and helpers.

18 State services

The Ministry of Planned Economy operates the work areas for basic supply and luxury supply in cooperation with the Social Villagers. The Ministry of Education is responsible for the operation of the educational institutions, the Ministry of Health for the operation of the hospital. The Ministry of Infrastructure is responsible for providing technical and material support for the construction and maintenance of roads, pipelines and buildings, while the Ministry of Media Affairs is responsible for operating the studio and broadcasting the radio and television programmes produced in the Social Village. The Ministry of Digital Affairs is responsible for creating and operating the intranet sites for Social Villages and newly established companies in cooperation with the Social Villagers. The Ministry of Innovation accompanies research or development projects, the establishment of Innovation Companies and the construction and operation of People's Innovation Companies, as well as the national and international marketing of industrial property rights and other innovations. The Ministry of Labour places entrepreneurs in the various

144Ministry of Security - 6 People's Protection Service

economic forms and provides auditing and advice through the Company Auditing Agency for companies in both work areas. It supports Experimental Enterprises in setting up and entering the market in other economic forms. The Ministry of Family Affairs promotes neighbourhood relations and runs family counselling centres, houses for children and houses for disabled people. The Ministry of Integration organises language and culture courses for asylum seekers. The Ministry of Finance administers the digital currency, which is paid out to the Social Card via the People's Bank and can only be spent on goods and services in the Social Village.

18.1 Division of responsibilities and buildings

The ministries provide services that are divided into different areas of accountability and buildings. Houses form the living and working space in the Social Village, centres ensure the supply. Staff from other ministries can live in the Social Village or in the surrounding area. If they live in the Social Village, their wages are lower because all working hours in the service of basic supply count towards their compulsory hours. This covers the expenses for housing, food, clothing, hygiene and health. In addition, the wage is paid in the currency of the Social Market Economy.

18.1.1 Town hall

The town hall is a building with the same facilities as all other town halls and is operated by the Ministry of State Organisation. All ministries have an office here and an elected deputy minister. The ministries are responsible for service delivery in their specialist department in the Social Village. The ministries are responsible for the equipment and training of staff needed to provide services.

Administration is administered digitally wherever possible. The use of staff and paper has to be approved by a majority of Social Villagers. Town hall staff not provided by the ministries work in the basic supply work area.

The town hall does not have its own plenary hall for decision-making. The direct democratic management of the Social Village takes place in the Municipal Hall in cooperation with the Social Villagers.

18.1.2 Security centre

The building at the entrance to the Social Village houses the security centre. It houses the Police Station, Fire Station, Bank, Municipal Court and Social Service. The building has a gate where persons entering or leaving the Social Village are controlled. Identity cards are also kept, issued and handed out at the gate. A police officer, a People's Protection Service officer and a Social Service officer staff the gate 24 hours a day. The police station contains detention cells and an armoury. Uniforms for police and fire service are kept in a large locker room. The police are supported by the People's Protection Service, which consists of Social Villagers.

The fire station houses fire engines and special operations equipment. The fire brigade is organised by Social Villagers in the work area basic supply. Exercise and duty hours are counted towards compulsory working hours. The Ministry of Security is responsible for equipment and training. The Ministry of Planned Economy is responsible for the Social Service.

In the reception area of the gate there is a People's Bank ATM where you can make transfers, change money, invest, withdraw or deposit money. As it is not possible to pay with cash in the Social Village, money is booked onto the social card at this machine. The People's Bank ATM is the responsibility of the Ministry of Finance. Deposits of foreign currencies and precious metals are taken over by the Social Service and brought to the nearest People's Bank branch.

The legal process is open to all Social Villagers.[145] There is a lay judge's court for settling disputes, whose lay judges are Social Villagers who have been selected at random and who perform the lay judge's service as compulsory working hours. Plaintiffs and defendants are each allowed to bring 2 Social Villagers

---

145 Ministry of Justice - 5.4 Courts

as lawyers. The only legally qualified employees are the prosecutors and judges. The legally knowledgeable staff must show the Social Villagers the affected paragraphs in the laws. The Ministry of Justice maintains the Municipal Court and sends offenders to the prisons or to the court hearings of the second instance. All instances are covered by the legal expenses insurance[146] , through which Planned Economy residents and companies are insured. It is financed from business taxes and is connected to compulsory work in the luxury supply work area. This is to pay off the premium costs if one cannot raise them from one's private assets. The loser bears the costs of the proceedings.

18.1.3 Health centre[147]

The health centre has technical equipment to perform operations and treatments on humans and animals and to produce medicines. The health centre is run by the Ministry of Health. It is a combination of pharmacy, hospital and specialist centre, similar to polyclinics in the former German Democratic Republic (GDR). It is open to all Social Villagers at all times. Emergencies come to the emergency room and other cases come during the given opening hours. Physicians and care workers take turns with the services in the surgeries and the hospital. This is to spread the workload and shift work equally. The professionals draw up the duty roster on their own, but each professional has a working hours account for outpatient or inpatient service and is entitled to a balanced working hours account. The maximum working time of 12 hours per day may not be exceeded.

The building has at least 2 operating theatres, a delivery room, 4-bed rooms, treatment rooms for the emergency room, medical practices for teeth, throat, nose, ears, eyes, skin, orthopaedics, heart, lungs, gastrointestinal and reproductive organs, and a pharmacy. The pharmacy dispenses Planned Economy medicines and produces specially adapted medicines for patients.

---

146 Ministry of Justice - 5.7.7 Legal expenses insurance
147 §236,9,10 Health care: BV Art. 117a

Benefits from Immortality Health Insurance[148] are not part of medical health care. It is possible to take out supplementary insurance if you have sufficient income and then, if necessary, it is linked to a transfer to a university hospital. The hospitals are specialised in the treatment of various diseases. Sick people may have to be transferred or move in order to receive the special treatment. If necessary, university hospitals are also used.

Medical services for physical or mental ailments are treated at the health centre. A cap is not provided for, but can be introduced in a plenary assembly for a limited period of time. All preventive medical check-ups are basic supply services.

18.1.4 Leisure Centre

A recreational park stretches along the various schoolyards via the sports facilities to the village square. Social Villagers can visit the Leisure Centre at any time and it is free of charge. The facilities are supervised and cared for by staff from the basic supply work area. They receive special training for this from staff of the Ministry of Family Affairs.

Expenditure on playground equipment in schoolyards and nursery schools is combined and supplemented by the Ministry of Family Affairs. The recreational park is a mixture of playground for young and old, fairground and adventure park with large rides. The attractions and rides are different in each Social Village. The residents of a Social Village have the right to determine which attractions are to be built in the new building. The ministries of education, family and infrastructure pay for the construction and maintenance of the recreational facilities as part of their recreational benefits.[149] The Social Villagers build the small attractions in cooperation with the Social Villages' craft enterprises. Large rides or attractions are financed from profits of Planned Businesses and Planned Enterprises and the saved annual tax revenues, which are distributed to all schools as scheduled to provide

---

148 Ministry of Health - 5.12.4 Immortality Health Insurance
149 Ministry of Education - 5.7 Buildings, Ministry of Family Affairs - 9.5 Playgrounds, Ministry of Infrastructure - 4.6 Leisure

playground equipment in playgrounds.

The Leisure Centre facilities blend seamlessly with the sports facilities. The playground equipment and scaffolding in the schoolyard and the swimming pool are used for instructional and recreational purposes. Each Leisure Centre also has a climbing park, a Ferris wheel and a swimming pool. The swimming pool is supported by district heating from the biogas plant. All pools are heated and specialised for splashing children, water sports or physiotherapy by water jet or waterfall. A comprehensive massage of the body through water is possible in a whirlpool landscape. The swimmers' pool allows water polo, high diving and lane swimming. The children's pool has a slide and a water mushroom. The Planned Business Leisure Centre operates the sports facilities in the Social Village and ensures that the Education Centre can use the sports facilities for sports lessons, the companies can use them for company sports and the Social Villagers can use them for leisure activities. The sports facilities consist of at least a sports hall, a sports field, a trim trail and climbing trees planted around the sports field. The Ministries of Labour, Education, Family, Infrastructure and Health pool their spending on sports opportunities for Social Villagers by providing suitable equipment for the sports facilities.[150]

18.1.5 Energy Centre[151]

The Energy Centre is operated by the Ministry of Infrastructure. It is used to pump groundwater and treat wastewater. It administers and maintains the well and the energy plants consisting of solar panels and wind turbines on the roofs, as well as the sewage treatment plant and biogas plant. Ideally, Social Villages are built along rivers in order to be able to operate water sports and hydroelectric power plants, as well as to have access to water transport routes.

The energy centre building houses the sewage treatment and

---

150 Ministry of Health - 6.2 Exercise, Ministry of Infrastructure - 4.6 Leisure, Ministry of Family Affairs - 9.3Sport, Ministry of Education - 8.7.4.8Sport, 9.15.2.3Sport.
151 §220.5 Agriculture

biogas plant as well as a kiln, turbine and dynamo. The sewage treatment plant treats wastewater from the sewage system and feeds the biogas plant with all animal and human faeces from the Social Village. Together with other vegetable and animal waste, the faeces are converted into methane and compost. The methane is burned with residual waste and used to generate electricity and district heating. The compost is given to farmers and gardeners. Combustible waste that cannot be recycled is burned in the kiln with the methane and converted into electricity. Via heat exchangers, the waste heat produced during the electricity generation process is sent to the buildings of the Social Village as district heating.

The well that supports the Social Village with drinking water is operated in another building. If there is no clean groundwater on the site, the Ministry of Infrastructure provides a connection to the nearest well and transfers it to the Social Village.

The Social Village has its own networks for electricity, information, drinking water and sewage. In areas where drinking water is scarce, drinking water is supplied through separate pipes that support each house with an indoor well that the house residents can help themselves to.

18.1.5.1 Power supply

There are solar panels and wind turbines on the roofs and facades of the Social Village buildings. All installations are administered and maintained by the staff of the Ministry of Infrastructure. The skilled workers travel around the Social Villages to carry out repairs or installations. All other work is to be done by Social Villagers in the basic supply work area. Training at the Education Centre may be required for the work. The electricity generated is fed into the domestic electricity network. Social Villages dispose of the kilowatt hours they generate themselves and are allowed to sell surplus electricity that they cannot store in their pumped-storage power stations.

18.1.6 House for disabled people[152]

The house for disabled people is a mixture of a home for disabled people and a barrier-free residence. Disabled people of all ages live there. Disabled children can also live in the children's house. Depending on the degree of disability and the number of caring relatives present, more or fewer social workers are employed in the house for disabled people. Family carers can take further training at the Education Centre and do all their compulsory working hours as social workers for disabled care by caring for several disabled people.

If there are not enough disabled people in a Social Village to fill a house, disabled people are placed in the Children's House and the Senior Citizens' House. At the health centre, it is determined what work each disabled person can do. The disabled then have priority for work that they can do. This applies to services in the basic supply work area and to Planned Enterprises.

18.1.7 Children's house[153]

All children living inland may decide for themselves at any time whether they want to live with their parents or in the children's home. Regardless of whether they live until they reach the age of majority, or just for a day, the children's home looks after all needy children around the clock. Children and youths can make use of every care offer in the Social Village with their Social Card. Care is offered around the clock at the Children's House, plus weekdays at the nursery schools and schools and on days off at the recreation park. Families can make use of parenting support services at the Children's House. Corresponding paragraphs of the Eighth Social Code are used as a template for determining the scope of assistance for parenting.[154] If children have to be taken into state custody because their parents are endangering the child's welfare[155] ,

---

152 §229,2,4 Unemployment, old-age, survivors' and disability benefits: BV Art. 111, §231,2 Integration of disabled persons: BV Art.112b
153 §43,2 Social rights: KV Art.29
154 http://www.gesetze-im-internet.de/sgb_8/
155 Ministry of Justice - 8.4.4 Child welfare endangerment

they are brought to the Children's Home by the police and the Social Service collects the children's belongings.

The children's house is a mixture of children's home, nursery school and playground. On the upper floors are the residents' children's rooms. On the lower floors are the age-appropriate playrooms with different toys. The residents are allowed to take all toys into their children's rooms to play with them themselves. To avoid excess, there is a cupboard for toys in each children's room. It may be filled to the brim, but otherwise there must be no more toys in the room. As soon as the children move out or get older, the toys go back into the playrooms. Two trained social workers live in the children's house. They receive as many workers from the basic supply work area per day as they need and can instruct. Workers are ordered from the Social Village's town hall. If more social workers are needed, they are ordered from the Ministry of Family Affairs.

For the youths, there is a garden hut, a tree house and a fireplace in the garden. The basement of the children's house is the air-raid shelter of the Social Village. It has 6 large rooms, sanitary facilities and a strong ventilation system with air filters. In one large room there are only folding beds, which fill 5 rooms. Since the air-raid shelter is never used if possible, children and youths are allowed to be as loud as they want there around the clock. 3 rooms can be booked by all Social Villagers through the Social Service. At weekends, at least one room serves as a disco.

18.1.8 Education Centre[156]

The Education Centre has teaching resources to provide all basic training for housing, food, clothing, hygiene and health. The Education Centre consists of several buildings that house the various educational institutions. These are nursery school, primary school, comprehensive school and college. Depending on the size of the buildings, nursery school and primary school as well as comprehensive school and college are combined.

156§45.2 Welfare state: BV Art.41, §177.6 Education: BV Art. 62

The Education Centre has chairs, tables, blackboards, computers, beamers, writing and drawing tools, special rooms with a fund of special devices and instruments for music, theatre, handicrafts, biology, chemistry, physics and computer science.

The Education Centre also houses the state-run special schools[157] , where disabled people are also educated and accompanied by their carers from the house for disabled people. All educational institutions have an outdoor area which they share. At the same time, this outdoor area is permanently used for recreational purposes by all Social Villagers. It extends between the buildings of the educational institutions to the sports facilities and the village square.

18.1.8.1 Childcare

The educational institutions support the children from the first year of life until the age of majority. Parents can agree on the hours of care with their children and the educational institutions. Compulsory school attendance applies from the age of 6 to 18.

18.2 Education policy[158]

The education policy in the Social Village is aimed at educating children and adults so that they do not become unemployed. Children receive the standard school education that is common throughout the country. Adults can catch up on all educational qualifications and attend vocational, further and advanced training courses. All types of schools are united in the education centres, and colleges specialise in the companies at the location. The Ministry of Planned Economy reports to the Ministry of Education which specialisation is available in which Social Village, so that skilled workers can be trained locally. Further education and training measures are offered for the qualification of volunteers. Digital education

---

157 Ministry of Education - 6 Special school

158 §181,3 Vocational education and training, §180,6,7 Schools and colleges: KV Art.44

supports learners through the Knowledge Directory and training glasses.[159]

Learners in the Education Centres take on tasks for Planned Economy companies by outsourcing work processes to the Education Centre and making them part of the teaching, as well as regular visits of learners to companies to work. This cooperation between education and supply is further extended to include research. Companies can give research assignments to Planned Economy colleges, but in return they have to participate in research studies and take tests that the researchers give them.

18.2.1 Education and training as work for basic supply[160]

Anyone who completes training in a subject with a shortage of skilled workers outside of compulsory education receives half an hour of working hours credited as compulsory work for each hour of instruction. Those who drop out of the training must work the credited working hours.

18.2.2 Visitation rights

Any Social Villager may attend any primary school, comprehensive school or college class without having to register. These visits are considered leisure activities, but the lessons may not be disturbed. The teachers decide whether the lessons are disturbed. If there is not enough space available, only learners registered for a degree may stay. Sufficient space must always be provided for them.

Every Social Villager is allowed to use the premises of the Education Centre when they are not occupied. Rooms are booked with the Social Service. For this purpose, the digital occupancy plan of the rooms is available in the Social Directory. Social Villagers can register there, if necessary in a waiting list.

---

159 Ministry of Education - 12.4 Digitised education
160 §182.1 Further education: BV Art. 64a

18.2.3 Knowledge communities

Social Villagers can give each other courses to share their qualifications with others. Those who want to offer a course sign up for a list of when and where they will share their knowledge. In the Social Village there are always free rooms at any time because 10% surplus must be kept. The Social Service takes care of the room allocation. At the beginning of each course, skills, goals and ideas of all group members are listed. This is how a course initially finds out who can help whom, who aims to do what with the knowledge and how the knowledge should best be imparted. In the Knowledge Directory, all courses can be accessed as a filmed video. Besides the video, additional materials are possible, such as screen presentation, handout, written elaboration and references to literature and online sources.

18.2.4 Further education

Any Social Villager who wishes to improve their skills can first be tested and then trained. For testing, exams are taken in the specified subjects. This is first done through a test in the Knowledge Directory[161] , where mock exams record the level of knowledge and sources of errors. What knowledge is missing and which courses in which educational institutions tie in with the knowledge level are displayed after the test. The Social Villager can register directly with the events and attend them or learn the lesson in the Knowledge Directory. The final exams of all teaching units must be successfully passed in the educational institution in order to obtain the degree.

If necessary, the examinee's duty roster for his or her compulsory work in the basic supply work area will be adjusted for the class attendance or the examination date. If teaching periods overlap with duty periods in the basic supply work area, teaching shall have priority. The total amount of compulsory work in the work area basic supply is not reduced by this, unless it is a further training to become a skilled worker with a shortage of skilled workers.

---

161 Ministry of Education - 12.7.4 Assessment Test

All examination dates for all subjects are published in the Education Directory on the page of the respective comprehensive or college. Anyone wishing to take part must register there at least one day in advance via their profile in the Persons Directory.

18.2.5 Training forecast

To ensure that no training ends in unemployment, it is determined before the start of the training[162] whether companies in the vicinity need workers with these qualifications after graduation or whether setting up a company in the desired area offers opportunities for profit due to sufficient demand. The training company must indicate a probability of whether the trainee will be taken on after the training and on what factors this depends. The trainee must ask for this data during the interview and enter it in his or her profile in the Education Directory. The algorithm mainly uses data from the Labour Directory, Education Directory and the Company Auditing Agency to match the number of companies and their turnover in the market with current and completed trainings. The migration of workers between the location of training, residence and employment, as well as occupational decisions away from the skills learned, are included in the probability calculation. The probability indicates how strongly other workers with the same qualifications will compete for the available jobs. Individual data of persons or companies are not published. In the end, there is a probability that in a given area, certain areas, the whole country or the whole world this training can be used profitably. The probabilities of the whole world are very inaccurate in the short term. Provided that in the long run the united states of the world share their data sets democratically, the predictions become more accurate.

162Ministry of Digital Affairs - 15.3 Algoracle

18.2.6 Study

All Social Villages offer training in their colleges to provide housing, food, clothing, hygiene and health. Studies at the Planned Economy colleges are always part-time, no matter which course is offered. Every study programme in the Social Village includes internships during all semester breaks in all companies related to the subject area.

The teaching and timetable is coordinated in voting with the local companies. Theoretical instruction is self-study via the Knowledge Directory or in the classrooms of the colleges. The examinations are taken in the classrooms of the colleges.

All the subject areas of the state colleges are available in all the Social Villages in the country. To study a desired subject, one probably has to move to another Social Village. The college in a Social Village offers only a few subject areas. The subject areas are linked to the companies that are present in the work areas of the Social Village. In addition, there are subject areas matching the specialisation of the location, so that in-service training is possible for all degrees. College students who attend subject areas in different Social Villages for their studies may move several times.

18.2.7 External in-service training[163]

Apprenticeships with companies in the Social Market Economy and Free Market Economy are arranged through the Labour Directory, provided there is a vacancy for the Social Villager's desired training. If the resident gets the training, they can move out of the Social Village or stay in the Social Village and pay the Planned Economy company tax rate on their wages. If the training place is further than 10 kilometres away, the trainee may travel free of charge by state transport. The educational institution may be located in the Social Village or in the surrounding area. The residence may remain in the Social Village until the training is completed and the Social Villager finds a job in another economic form with which he/she can support him/herself.

---

163 §180.6 Schools and colleges: KV Art.44, §228.8 Labour: KV Art.39

18.2.8 Exchange programmes

At the schools, there is an exchange programme for school children from Planned Economy with school children and their families from Free Market Economy, Social Market Economy and Barter Economy.[164] Where they want to go is up to the children and youths themselves to decide. Cities, clubs, schools or universities can become exchange sponsors by placing children and youths from Social Villages with their own staff or members of their families. An exchange can last for different lengths of time. The length of time is decided voluntarily by the guests and hosts.

18.2.9 Training glasses

In the Planned Economy, all newcomers are introduced to their compulsory work for basic supply for one week with the training glasses[165] . If more workers are needed at short notice, many Social Villagers can help quickly without having to go through training first. If the training glasses detect a work error, the person wearing the glasses is asked to correct it or to wait until a competent person is on site.

18.3 Employment exchange[166]

Advice on employment exchange to the Barter Economy or market economy can be obtained at the Town Hall in the office of the Ministry of Labour.[167] Alternatively, this employment exchange can be done through the Labour Directory. The focus is on the interest of the worker, regardless of qualifications. All jobs are displayed, sorted by sector, and how long it would take to obtain the necessary qualifications. The qualification can then be acquired in the Education Centre with the appropriate subject area in the Social Village. In the advice, the algorithm calculates how many vacancies require this qualification, how

---

164 Ministry of Education - 9.17 Student exchange
165 Ministry of Education - 12.4.1 Training glasses
166 §228,1c,8 Labour: BV Art. 110, KV Art.39
167 Ministry of Labour - 12.2.1 Employment exchanges

many workers with this qualification are already in the labour market, how many of them will soon retire and how many are in training at domestic educational institutions. The jobseeker can narrow down or expand the data set accessed by the algorithm and change his or her interests as desired.

18.3.1 Jobbus

The Social Service organises bus trips where companies in the same sector or with the same jobs are visited by jobseekers. In order for the job bus to set off, enough voluntary passengers must have been found. Social Villagers and other jobseekers can book the Job Bus on the Ministry of Labour's profile page in the State Directory. Each jobseeker will be invited via the Labour Directory when a bus is due to leave in their area, calling at companies they have listed in their profile as companies or jobs they are looking for. The bus timetable is available on the Ministry of Labour's profile page in the State Directory. Users can view the bus timetable, book seats and make proposals for stops. The timetable is based on the qualifications of the jobseekers travelling with them and companies seeking staff with the same qualifications.

As soon as there are enough commitments, the bus sets off on the agreed date. The companies specify the dates on which they could offer tours and the passengers choose the majority of suitable dates. The Ministry of Labour takes care of the company contacts and involves companies of all economic forms.

At the stops, passengers are given company tours and insights into jobs that are currently or will soon be vacant due to retirement, pregnancy or after the notice period. Company secrets are kept secret and visitors are not allowed to look at them.

Social Market Economy unemployment insured can also use this service. The Social Service receives foreign currency from the Ministry of Social Market Economy.

18.3.2 Career fair

There are regular job fairs in Social Villages. To these, the resident Employment Office invites searching companies from the market economy. Interested companies can present their goods and services at the job fair and thereby recruit voluntary new workers. Stands of the entrepreneurs can be built on the village square, in the community hall or in companies of Planned Economy. If work on special machines or with special techniques is to be shown and tried out, the stands are located in the corresponding companies.

The date of a job fair is always after the final exams have been taken at the Education Centre. The qualifications of the Social Villagers looking for work play a role in the selection of companies that are specifically invited. If a job-seeker lives in a Social Village, but a job fair with companies matching his or her qualifications is held in another Social Village, he or she is released from work in the work area of basic supply and luxury supply for a business trip.

18.3.3 Employer visits

Interested employers can observe potential workers at work in Planned Businesses, Centres and Planned Enterprises. These visits can be announced or unannounced. This is decided by the employees as soon as a request is received. Certainly, this is already an announcement, but the exact date can also be sometime in the future. The affected employees can choose whether they want to know the date, the time period or nothing at all. If a staff member decides not to know, the other staff members can ask for the date, but they must promise not to disclose it.

18.4 Media

The Ministry of Media Affairs provides auditory and audiovisual media production devices so that each Social Village can operate a radio station and a TV channel. The radio and television programmes are broadcast on the Social

Directory. The radio broadcaster also broadcasts via antenna on a locally receivable frequency. The TV channel broadcasts the programmes in the Nationwide Citizen Television[168] that have received the most positive ratings in the Social Directory. Depending on the content, the broadcasts are additionally included in a programme of the five state television stations. For the operation of the broadcasters, a fixed share of compulsory working hours is covered from the basic supply work area. Content is produced in the work area of luxury supply or in clubs and is only remunerated if customers from the market economy pay for it.

18.4.1 Contents

The Ministry of Media Affairs can provide training or advice on how content could be made appealing and legal. The right to make changes lies solely with the creators, censorship is prohibited. Content must be broadcast as submitted. Content that violates applicable law is inadmissible. The Ministry of Media Affairs checks the content for legal violations as soon as the video material has been uploaded to the Social Directory. Only after this check is the content released. In the case of a refusal, the affected offence must be reproduced in the law in the wording of the affected paragraph. The legal process is open to the author.

18.4.2 Radio

Social Village Radio plays music that residents have chosen and produced themselves, advertisements for jobs and new products from Innovation Enterprises and Experimental Enterprises, as well as reports by voluntary reporters and audio books. If the range of content is too large for one radio station, a total of up to five radio stations can be operated, each with its own frequencies.

Music requests that are subject to a fee must be published on the radio station's profile as a contribution. If enough Social

___
168 Ministry of Media - 11 Nationwide Citizen Television

Villagers rate the music request positively, the cover band of the Planned Economy is commissioned to create a cover song and purchase the rights for it. This purchase requires foreign currency. A budget for the purchase is set in the annual needs assessment. If no foreign currency is available, no chargeable music requests can be fulfilled.

The radio station also plays house music and announcements. There is a loudspeaker in the village square that plays the radio station at room volume. As soon as a public speech is made on this square, it is also broadcast on the radio.

18.4.3 Television

Each Social Village has the equipment to turn the community hall into a film or TV show studio. Voluntary Social Villagers can act as directors, actors, reporters, moderators and candidates and produce any format together.

A budget for the purchase of trademark rights is not provided. The filmmakers' unification is responsible for protecting and marketing the trademark rights of television productions. Provided it earns foreign currency from this, the filmmakers decide whether to pay out the money to the filmmakers, purchase devices or buy rights of use for audiovisual content.

There is a TV channel for each individual Social Village and for all Social Villages. It hosts feature films from the Social Village's educational institutions, shows on employment exchanges and business start-ups, finding work partners and finding employees. The employment exchange shows aim to bring together able and willing Social Villagers who want to start a company together.

In addition to the employment exchange show, there is also a show to find partners for other situations in life. What partners are sought for is decided by the applicants and the viewers, for example for sex, love, interests, clubs or other leisure activities. The mayor hosts a news programme every week with contributions from all the ministries in his Social Village. The content is to be the work of all politicians in the Social Village of the previous week. The news programme is broadcast on Saturday evenings so that the content can be discussed at the plenary assembly on Sunday.

18.4.4 Newspaper

The Social Village Newspaper is published in only one printed edition, which is publicly available in a display box in front of the town hall and digitally accessible in the Social Directory. The Ministry of Media Affairs office in the town hall is responsible for the notice boards. All Social Villagers can make submissions to the Social Directory or drop them off at the Ministry of Media Affairs office. The display boxes are placed in a circle with an opening so that they can be filled from the outside and inside. Right next to the newspaper display boxes is the notice board, which is made up of display boxes in a circle of the same design. Social Villagers can post requests, offers, letters to the editor or appeals here. At the top of the showcases are cameras that are pointed at the showcases so that the content can be displayed directly in the Social Directory via webcam.

18.5 Asylum

The Ministry of Integration operates the asylum houses and is responsible for the initial reception procedure.[169] With their asylum houses, the Social Villages provide the initial reception facilities for asylum seekers. Here it is decided within 6 months whether the asylum seekers move to the Asylum Village[170] or are accepted as refugees in a host family[171] of the other economic forms. If the Ministry of Foreign Affairs recognises the country of origin as safe within the first 6 months, deportation will take place. A maximum of 10% of the residents of a Social Village may be asylum seekers, after which there is a freeze on admissions. The capacities are automatically retrieved via the Social Directory and reported to the Ministry of Foreign Affairs. As soon as an admission freeze becomes unavoidable in all Social Villages, the Ministry

---

169 Ministry of Integration - 8.4.5 Initial reception
170 Ministry of Integration - 8.6.1 Asylum Village
171 Ministry of Integration - 8.5.1 Host family

of Foreign Affairs must instruct the embassies[172] not to accept any more asylum applications.

18.5.1 Asylum houses

Only asylum seekers who speak the same language are to live in the asylum house. The language groups are distributed nationwide. A maximum of one foreign language should be spoken per Social Village. If there are more different languages of the asylum seekers than Social Villages, there may also be two languages. Since asylum seekers are only allowed to stay in the Social Village for 6 months, many moves have to be made. Asylum seekers do this work for each other in the work area basic supply with the help of the Social Service.

18.5.2 Sponsors

Each asylum seeker is assigned a sponsor. Sponsors are Social Villagers who commit themselves in the duty roster for 6 months to look after the asylum seeker for 7 hours a week. Sponsors ensure that the asylum seekers find their way around and complete their compulsory work. Asylum seekers who do not complete their compulsory work are threatened with deportation if they receive repeated warnings. Sponsors help asylum seekers find skilled workers who explain how to do the compulsory work in addition to guiding them through the training glasses. If no expertise is required, the godparents receive training glasses and see the contributions in the national language. Then they demonstrate the work to their asylum seeker. The sponsors invite their asylum seekers to participate in plenary assemblies or to join clubs. Asylum seekers do not have voting rights at the plenary assembly, but they do have the right to speak if they have an interpreter.

---

172 Ministry of Foreign Affairs - 9.2 Asylum application in embassies

18.5.3 Interpreters and teachers

The teachers who teach the national language as a foreign language to the refugees in the Education Centre are also interpreters for the language of the asylum seekers. If this qualification is not readily available, recourse is made to appropriate linguists in the educational institutions and, if possible, to digital translation programmes. Interpreting services are used in the classroom and in the companies or enterprises. The sponsors are allowed to ask interpreters for help, but have to wait for an appointment if demand is high. In addition, multilingual persons are sought among the asylum seekers who speak the same foreign language as some Social Villagers. An automatic search for interpreters can be carried out in the Social Directory because all users import their data from the Persons Directory or Asylum Directory and indicate their foreign language skills there.[173]

18.5.4 Basic supply for asylum seekers

Asylum seekers receive training glasses to enable them to carry out the activities of the work area basic supply. Instructions are translated once into their language and are then available in the Knowledge Directory of the Internet[174] . This enables asylum seekers who have been inland to teach their compatriots how to carry out basic supply activities for housing, food, clothing, health and hygiene after they return home. All asylum seekers receive this basic training in the first 6 months of their presence inland to prepare them for work in the Asylum Village. In principle, Asylum Villages are structured in the same way as Social Villages, but they only have the work area of basic supply and the necessary training courses in the Education Centre. Other subject areas are not offered at the colleges in the Asylum Villages. They learn the direct democratic way of working and governing through their own experience in the Planned Economy.

------

173 Ministry of Education - 5.9 Education Directory, Ministry of Integration - 8.3 Asylum Directory
174 Ministry of Digital Affairs - 10.2.1 Knowledge.dir

18.5.5 Luxury supply for asylum seekers

Asylum seekers are only allowed to work in the luxury supply work area, which is designated for house construction, and receive the necessary training at the Education Centre. In addition, they receive instruction on domestic criminal law and their rights for residence, freedom of movement and co-determination. All teaching content is translated once. If asylum seekers notice faulty translations in the lessons, they report the faults so that the teacher can improve them.

18.5.6 Moves of asylum seekers

The moves of the asylum seekers are carried out by the old neighbours in the Social Village and the new neighbours in the Asylum Village or the host family and the Social Service. Asylum seekers are invoiced for the removal costs right at the beginning. If they cannot pay these costs, they have to work them out in the work area luxury supply.

19 Mobile Social Villages

There are mobile Social Villages consisting of containers. Container cross modules[175] can be used to build homes, centres and companies on any open space. This makes it possible to adapt flexibly and quickly to fluctuations in demand and supply capacities locally. Container cross modules can also be placed individually next to fixed buildings to support supply during the construction period. An entire Social Village can be built on the former company site in the event of the bankruptcy of a large local employer with over 10,000 employees.

Mobile Social Villages become particularly necessary when Planned Economy becomes fashionable or world economic crises, national disasters of a natural or economic nature arise. The containers are stored in an erected state so that they can be used by Social Villagers. At the same time as they are used, maintenance is ensured by the users during compulsory working hours. As soon as the containers have to be used to compensate for capacity bottlenecks in a Social Village,

---

175Ministry of Infrastructure - 5.9 Mobile City

they are relocated. Once the new buildings are constructed, the move from the containers to the buildings takes place. In addition to increasing capacity during construction, the containers make an important contribution to being able to support supplies in the event of a disaster or war.

20 Disaster management[176]

The Ministries of Security and Planned Economy develop different emergency plans for different scenarios, which they present to the people in a committee. The emergency plans are adapted to the will of the people and rehearsed. After the rehearsal, the citizens vote whether they agree with the emergency plan as it is or whether it should be adjusted and rehearsed again. The adjustment and rehearsal can be repeated as many times as necessary until majority approval is achieved. Because Social Villages have a significant role in disaster management, their residents need to rehearse more scenarios more frequently. Through this increased rehearsal, Social Villagers become trainers and briefers for the rest of the population in the event of a disaster, when they have to move to the Social Village or switch the entire population to Planned Economy until the disaster is dealt with. The Ministry of Planned Economy reorganises production in the Social Villages as much as necessary to ensure basic supply of food, clothing, building materials, electricity and water for the affected people. The Ministry of Security is primarily responsible for the implementation of all measures and legislation in disaster management.[177]

20.1 Case of war

In the event of war, the Social Villages are again used as barracks. The People's Protection Service soldiers move into the barracks and vulnerable Social Villagers, for example disabled people or children, move into the soldiers' flats. All other Social Villagers can stay there, but now have to share

---

176 §211,1,3,4 National supply: BV Art. 102
177 Ministry of Security - 5.7 Disaster management

fewer rooms with each other. The capacity limits are fully utilised and supported by mobile Social Villages. All Social Villagers switch luxury supply to war economy.

21 Switching to the new system

The welfare state principle is fundamentally reformed. The payment of money is discontinued. Benefits in kind and jobs are offered to establish basic supply. In a phase of mobilisation, all unemployed, volunteers and former soldiers are used to convert all barracks into Social Villages. This is followed by plenary assemblies with needs assessments and roster allocations.

21.1 Retention of child benefit

The only exception to transfer payments is child benefit, which from now on will be charged to the children's social cards. This can be used to pay for care facilities for minors where the children are staying.

21.2 Establishment of basic support

Basic welfare services are taken over by Planned Economy and provided in places in buildings owned by the state. This eliminates transfer payments, such as cash payments for housing, utilities, parents or trainings.

The housing allowance is no longer necessary because the Social Villages provide housing. Social welfare for support becomes unnecessary because Social Villagers work out their basic supply themselves collectively in their compulsory working hours.

The parental allowance is transferred to the child benefit because parents are approved by the increased child benefit and may decide in the first two years of a child's life whether they look after the child themselves or have the child looked after in an institution. If the parents decide to care for their child themselves, the child benefit is transferred to their children's account.

Cash benefits to trainees become unnecessary because attendance at all state schools and colleges is free. In addition, every course of study is offered in the colleges of the Social Villages that is also offered at the rest of the state colleges.

21.3 Transfer of compulsory insurances

Compulsory insurances are transferred to insurances offered by the ministry of the Social Market Economy and are only obligatory for companies of the Social Market Economy. Namely, these are unemployment insurance, long-term care insurance, health insurance, pension insurance and accident insurance. Free Market Economy companies can also offer these and other insurances. However, the state does not assume any liability for default on payment or insolvency.

21.4 Dissolution of the pay-as-you-go system

The statutory pension insurance from the pay-as-you-go system leads to the pension in the Social Village. Current contributions are transferred to the Social Market Economy pension insurance or paid out. The pay-as-you-go system is abolished. Unfortunately, since the abolition happened too late, it has to happen suddenly now. Morally, however, this is appropriate, because the generations that had the few children and accumulated the debts are currently of retirement age. If they do not pay now for their mismanagement, the pay-as-you-go system will become increasingly unfair for future generations. Those who have not made sufficient private provision will have to move to the Social Village. Those who have fathered and raised at least three children will be exempt from the rule and will be paid the statutory pension until death.

21.5 Capacity planning

How many residents the Social Villages will have will be determined in the beginning. In the short term, all persons who need immediate support must move into the Social Villages as soon as possible. These are all current welfare recipients and humans who supplement their income with social benefits in order to survive.

In the medium term, volunteers will also want to live in Planned Economy. The number of volunteers will be determined by registering on the ministry's website for Planned Economy. Volunteers who would like to live in Planned Economy can report on the website.

In the long term, the size and number of building areas should be such that unemployment of 20% can be absorbed. The buildings will only be built when they are needed, but the dimensions of the building areas are already designed for centres and houses to be raised, extended and newly built.

21.6 Introduction of the Planned Economy

To coordinate services until the first needs assessment can be held, old documents from the German Democratic Republic (GDR) planning authority are used to determine the demand for the first year. Through the Social Village Directory, the GDR plan codes are made available to Social Villagers for election. In this way, the unemployed can choose where they want to work as long as there is no shortage of another job. Transfer is only possible if the family situation allows it and the necessary qualifications cannot be found elsewhere.

21.7 Social Village Directory

The Social Village Directory is the Internet version of the later Social Directory of the Intranet. It contains functions that are no longer available in the later Social Directory and does not yet contain all the functions of the later Social Directory. It is used for initial elections, voting and decision-making processes.

21.8 Mobilisation

In the mobilisation phase, all measures of social assistance recipients are terminated unless the social assistance recipient asks to be allowed to complete a further training measure. All welfare recipients must report to the nearest Employment Office or Job Centre at 7:50 a.m. on weekdays. From there, they are picked up by Social Service buses and trucks and taken to the nearest Social Village for repair and move-in. Mobilisation is completed once all the following steps have been taken.

21.8.1 Visit

The first trip from the Employment Office to the Social Village is to visit the Social Village and to describe the contents of the service for the coming months.

On the outward journey, tablet PCs are used to create their own profile in the Social Village Directory and a profile for all family members. Then a survey is made in which social welfare recipients indicate how many persons they are moving with, how many cubic metres of property need to be transported and how long it takes them to finish packing everything. Moving dates are given in a doodle voting.[178]

In the future Social Village, the social welfare recipients get a guided tour of the entire barracks, i.e. all the open spaces, rooms, furnishings, tools and machines. It is explained what will be built where in the future and what it will be used for.

On the way back, a survey is made as to which house and room the welfare recipients would like to live in. The barracks visited are digitally recreated. The planned uses of the rooms are indicated there. However, social welfare recipients can make new allocations in the survey themselves and put them to a digital voting among all future neighbours.

The survey can be viewed at any time via the Social Village Directory profile. The cubic metre number of belongings must be definitively stated one week before pickup, as well as the number of moving boxes. The new flat must be virtually

---

178 https://doodle.com/de/

furnished one week before the pickup. Own furniture is 3D standard templates, the dimensions of which can be deformed to indicate the actual size of the furniture carried. Those who do not have furniture available can have furniture provided by the army. This furniture must be moved from the 3D digital warehouse to the new digital flat. The new digital flat must be set up by one week before pickup so that everything is ready upon arrival. All welfare recipients are entitled to receive empty supermarket packing boxes as moving boxes.

21.8.2 Moving date

An algorithm calculates the optimal routes and collection times from the removal dates given in the survey. The welfare recipients are given these dates and must have everything packed in boxes by this time. All furniture that can be taken down must be dismantled, all furniture, compartments and drawers must be empty. A bulky waste collection comes the day before the pickup.

21.8.3 Pickup

The Social Service takes care of the move. As many trucks as necessary come to take the specified number of cubic metres in one trip. Army trucks and buses of different sizes drive in the column. Once a truck or bus is full, it goes to the Social Village. About 3 to 4 households are picked up together. Everyone helps. The first household to be hit is the one with the least number of cubic metres. The drivers of the trucks and buses load the belongings together with the welfare recipients. At the last household to be reached, all the occupants of the bus help to put away all the belongings. All moving boxes are taped shut with special tape to seal them.

21.8.4 Arrival

All the items are unloaded one after the other by all the welfare recipients in a column together and placed in the new flats. The new neighbours are already assigned to help place and assemble furniture.

21.8.5 Conversion

Until a Social Village is ready for occupancy, the unemployed live in the dilapidated but harmless dwellings, mostly old barracks or industrial sites in their own furniture or in furniture provided by the army. Gradually, first the centres, then the dwellings and then the companies' buildings are refurbished, built and furnished.

21.8.6 Voluntary service

All voluntary participants in the mobilisation can take part in the construction of the Social Villages, not only social welfare recipients. Volunteers have to create a profile on the website of the social welfare office. There they indicate their qualifications and can choose which work they would like to do. They are fed while they work, but are only given a place to live when all the unemployed or top-up workers have been accommodated. Only when the Social Village is ready can volunteers also move into the Planned Economy.

21.8.7 Former soldiers

During the conversion of all the barracks into Social Villages, former soldiers are the ushers for the incoming social welfare recipients. The workers are told what work they are to do by the marshals. The ushers receive their instructions from an architectural office commissioned by the Minister of Planned Economy, if there are no architectural offices of the Ministry of Infrastructure by then. Instructors do the initial scheduling of welfare recipients, depending on their stated qualifications.

Work is divided into Construction Service, Supply Service, Kitchen Service, Cleaning Service, Medical Service, Washing Service, Moving Service and Social Service. After mobilisation, the duty roster is drawn up democratically.

After the referral activities are completed, follow-up contracts are offered. The ex-servicemen can either stand guard at the Social Village gate in the Security Centre, work at the Social Service, or they can transfer to the Ministry of Security to join the People's Protection Service, the Police or the Continental Defence Army Corps, or move into the Social Village themselves and take another educational qualification.

21.8.8 Restoration of the barracks

Together with the ushers, the buildings are all put back into shape. It is not about beauty here, but about functionality. The interior walls can still be painted if the Social Village provides the basic supply. First and foremost, no buildings must be in danger of collapsing and must have electricity and water connections. The room layout of the rooms will remain the same for the time being. As soon as the Social Village guarantees the basic supply, the following plenary assembly will decide on the room layout in the dwellings and start interior work.

21.8.9 First aid from the army's central warehouse

Depending on the capacity of the army camps, the rooms in the barracks houses are furnished with army equipment or the welfare recipients who move in bring their own furniture. This has to be discussed with the referrers. For this purpose, a nationwide database must be established showing how many persons need living space, how many rooms are available in all domestic barracks, how much state-owned furniture, such as beds, cupboards, chairs and tables, there is in total in the army's central warehouses. The Social Service ensures the logistical distribution of furniture between central stores and barracks with the barracks' motor pools. All this information can be found in the Social Village Directory.

21.8.10 Gradual move of welfare recipients and top-up recipients

The move takes place step by step. As soon as a house is ready for occupancy, it is moved into. The more who live in the Social Village, the more who have a short way to work. Depending on how many social welfare recipients there are locally, they are distributed to surrounding barracks or the nearest barracks is expanded. However, if the barracks are to be expanded, the national capacity limit must first be reached. All old barracks must first be populated, then new buildings are constructed where many welfare recipients lived, so that these humans have a perspective of moving back to their old homeland if they still want to.

21.8.11 Schoolchildren

All school-age children of social welfare recipients attend surrounding schools during the mobilisation. There is a special bus service from the Social Village to all affected schools. This shuttle service is discontinued when all rooms and teachers of all class levels are operational at the Education Centre.

21.9 Conversion of the old ministries

For the conversion of the old ministries, all departments and units of the old ministries that are changing to this ministry are identified. The organigrams are used to determine whether an entire department and all its units are changing or only individual units. All unsuitable departments and units are dropped. The existing staff adapts its tasks to the new requirements.

Contact form

Dear reader
If you would like to make what you have read come true, in whole or in part, together with other like-minded people, I offer you several possibilities with this contact form. Fill it out, tear out the page and send it by post to:
Andreas Seidl, P.O. Box 1206, 63488 Seligenstadt / Germany

Or send the details to:
Phone: 0049 1522 818 2243 (whatsapp, telegram, signal)
Email: andreas.seidl2022@web.de

Please mark with a cross:
O   I want to found a dynamic People's Party.
O   I want to donate money for implementation.
O   I want contacts with like-minded people in my area.

Forename: _______________________________________

Surname: _______________________________________

Please fill in only the contact option through which a reply should be made.

Street, house no.: _______________________________

Postcode, city, country: __________________________

Phone: ____

Email address: __________________________________